HOME
IS THE SEA:
FOR WHALES

MARINELAND OF FLORIDA

Trained dolphins jumping through hoops (above)
and playing baseball (below)

MARINELAND OF FLORIDA

HOME
IS THE SEA:
FOR WHALES

By *Sarah R. Riedman and
Elton T. Gustafson*

ILLUSTRATED WITH PHOTOGRAPHS

Abelard-Schuman
London   New York   Toronto

Jacket front photograph from Marineland of Florida

LONDON	NEW YORK	TORONTO
Abelard-Schuman	*Abelard-Schuman*	*Abelard-Schuman*
Limited	*Limited*	*Canada Limited*
8 King St. WC2	*257 Park Ave. S.*	*228 Yorkland Blvd.*
	10010	*425*

Printed in the United States of America

An Intext Publisher

Contents

Illustrations

1

What About Whales?

THE DAY BEFORE Christmas, 1964, a dead whale drifted into New York harbor. Sighted whales, dead or alive, are always newsworthy because people never lose their curiosity about the largest animals ever to inhabit the earth—on land or in its waters. This one, a 50-foot fin whale weighing 42 tons, shared a prominent place in the newspapers and on radio and television with the last-minute pre-holiday items. In the *New York Times* the story was headlined: "BY LAND AND SEA, VISITORS FLOCK TO SEE DEAD WHALE."

As if "lying in state," tied up by its fluke (tail) at the end of a mile-long United States Army pier south of Jersey City, the majestic colossus, towed from the Hudson River by the Coast Guard, attracted throngs of visitors, the city fathers among them. After three days of public viewing, Army engineers consigned the giant to the bottom of the sea and dynamited its massive hulk. Big as it was, this specimen was not fully grown, because fin whales grow to 70 or 85 feet, depending upon whether they live in the Northern or Southern Hemisphere. Even at that size they rank second to the blue whale, which reaches a length of nearly 100 feet and weighs as many or more tons.

Tales, both true and imagined, are bound to be told whenever one of these Leviathans is encountered. When our finback— so identified by the curator of the New York Aquarium—turned up, a nine-year-old girl recalled reading about an old agreement between the Manhattan Indians and the colonists to share the oil of all whales washed ashore. Following this lead, the newspaper researchers dug up in the records of colonial days the provision

11

that all such finds became the property of the British Crown. According to then existing agreements, "A whale warden was appointed to look after such whales" and to take charge of distributing each part of the carcass.

At about the time that the final rites were given to the New York harbor fin, the City of Vancouver, British Columbia, was still mourning the loss of a killer whale that its inhabitants had taken to their hearts. As the story was told by David MacDonald in a lead article in *Rod & Gun,* March, 1965, a Canadian sculptor had been commissioned to kill a killer whale ". . . the fiercest thing that swims—and to make a model of it for an aquarium in Vancouver . . ." After two months of waiting, the sculptor succeeded in harpooning his life model, but lost heart just when he was about to pull the trigger and finish the capture. Perhaps his hand was stayed by the sight of two other killers that swam under their stunned companion and nudged it to the surface for a breath of air. Then the 3,000-pound whale was saved for a short three months of life as a captive celebrity.

Dr. Murray Newman, curator of the Vancouver Public Aquarium, was in charge of operations: towing the whale 40 miles from Saturna Island, arranging for a temporary home in a drydock where a fenced-off swimming pool was improvised, administering first aid to the harpoon wound, and giving the whale

Killer whale (*Orcinus orca*)

an injection of penicillin with a 12-foot hypodermic. A team of scientists—several biologists, a mammalogist, a dermatologist, and others—were on hand at the rescue. The surprisingly gentle beast was named Moby Doll. Then followed trying days of coaxing it to eat, and when Moby Doll downed her first fish, a loud cheer went up and the whole city drew a deep breath of relief.

The point of the story is that the capture of the killer roused world-wide interest among ordinary folk and scientists alike. They flew to Vancouver to tape its voice, test its intelligence, and film its graceful motions. It was reported that offers to purchase it for research in submarine design, echo-ranging, and human disease were made by renowned laboratory directors, but Vancouver would not give up its prize exhibit. Help came from many sources, including the Canadian Army and Navy and private shipbuilders, for manpower and supplies to build a suitable whale-pen. Navy frogmen and ordinary citizens alike donated their labor. Newspaper, radio, and television reports of its health were followed avidly. Many distinguished visitors, including two cabinet ministers and the Duke and Duchess of Windsor, came to view the "tiger of the sea" in its temporary home. A daily visitor was the sculptor whom Moby Doll adopted as a friend, and for whom she learned to roll over so that he could scratch her stomach with a brush. When he was not sitting with the whale, he was working on a life-sized model of her—his original commission.

Unfortunately, the story has a sad ending. Because of the low salt content of the water in the harbor where the Fraser River empties, the whale became ill and died before a permanent salt-water home could be built. Not only did the local press carry black headlines, but the London *Times* gave Moby a two-column obituary with the heading of the same size it ran at the outbreak of World War II. Countless letters of sympathy poured in to Moby's closest friends: Dr. Newman and the sculptor.

A surprise ending to the story was supplied by the post-mortem examination. You will read about it in Chapter 8.

And then on June 23, 1965, almost a year to the day after Moby Doll's capture, came Namu, male killer whale and the center of a news storm that was to rock the city of Seattle, the state of Washington, and the Pacific Coast all the way down from upper British Columbia, Canada.

A young Canadian fisherman, William Lechkobit, seining for salmon in Fitzhugh Sound at the mouth of the Bella Coola River, snagged his gill net on a reef and put in to the nearby canning village of Namu for the night. Early the next day, fellow fisherman Robert McGarvey happened by the reef and came upon the strangest catch in fishing history. During the night a pod of killer whales had moved in on the caught salmon and two of them were trapped in the net! One, a small calf, later escaped, but the big one, for some reason, stayed on.

The two fishermen knew that with Moby Doll dead they had a great prize, the only captive killer, but what could they do with it? They also knew that every day they kept their prize they would have to feed him 250 pounds of salmon! So they got on the telephone and spread the word that a killer whale was for sale. As soon as he heard about it, Edward I. "Ted" Griffin, director of the Seattle Public Aquarium, offered $8,000, with $500 as a down payment. It wasn't what the fishermen had expected, but it was the best offer, and they accepted. With cash donations in his pocket, Ted Griffin flew to Namu and closed the deal. The fishermen had lost a headache. Ted Griffin had a tiger by the tail.

In sufficient time he raised the rest of the money and had possession of the whale, but now what? What do you do with an animal more than 20 feet long and weighing probably more than 8,000 pounds?

Griffin arranged for many tons of iron to be flown in, welded it together with 41 empty oil drums, made a netting for the bottom and to fill in the sides, and with the help of 200 villagers lifted the 40x60x16 foot whale-pen into the water by hand: "It was then that we named the whale Namu, to thank those wonderful people for their help."

Killer whales rise from the water for a closer look at Namu

On July 8 the job was completed; Namu swam peacefully into the pen, and in only a few hours learned to swim with it in motion. But ahead lay some of the most treacherous water in the Pacific Coast—the wind-whipped rolling swells of Queen Charlotte Sound, the narrow channels of Johnstone Strait, the boiling whirlpools of Seymour Narrows, where huge freighters have sunk 100 fathoms before reaching the wide open stretches of the Strait of Georgia—and they made it!

The killers came, in pods of 30 or 40, and seemed to want to

Namu in his traveling whale-pen

Tug towing Namu

free Namu, but they didn't attack. A cow and two calves, assumed to be Namu's family, came close and whistled and shrieked, and Namu flicked his flukes a bit, but *never* tried to break out of the pen.

People were more dangerous! On July 13, "fanatic groups" tried to free the whale, and this was but one of several attempts. On July 16, the Canadian West Coast Fishermen's Union urged the government to impound Namu for Canada.

On July 21, Namu ate two salmon, his first food in eight days.

On July 24, Namu entered the United States and passed customs inspection, with flying colors, at Friday Harbor.

On July 27, Namu arrived at his new home in Seattle, to a thunderous welcome. Today, he can be seen there, a "handsome dapper whale" with his dorsal fin five feet high, and with "brilliant white rabbit-ear markings at each side of his massive head." Truly, the story is a saga of the sea.*

It is not surprising that primitive people were as awed as

* Unfortunately just before this book went to press Namu died, on July 9, 1966.

we are today by these enormous creatures. In history's strange records, dating back as far as 4,000 years, we find their forms carved in rock. Rocks in northern Norway tell the story in flint-scratched drawings that depict several tiny boats around a single huge whale. The bones of whales found in Alaska tell us that Eskimos must have caught whales close to shore at least 15 centuries B.C. The Greeks and Romans lived at peace with the whale, certainly with the large ones. They decorated vases, coins, and buildings with representations of dolphins, the smaller cousins in the whale family, and in their mythology wove many legends about them.

In modern times Thor Heyerdahl, who with his crew crossed the Pacific on the raft *Kon-Tiki,* wrote about their first sight of a whale:

A sound of snorting behind us, like that of a swimming horse, made us tremble. An enormous whale was staring at us, so close that we could see the inside of its blowhole, gleaming like a polished shoe. It was strange to hear something actually breathing in the sea, where all living creatures move in silence, without lungs, their gills quivering.

Whether they hunt whales for food and other rich materials to be taken from the mammoth carcasses, or whether as sightseers they travel thousands of miles to observe the parade of California gray whales during the annual migrations to their mating grounds, people everywhere are captivated by this remarkable family of animals. Thousands delight daily in the antics of trained dolphins, taught in "underwater universities" to perform feats of incredible power and coordination. And for stay-at-homes there is Flipper—with his several understudies—whose stunts enchant the show's directors as much as the millions of television viewers, and who was nominated by Cleveland Amory (June 12, 1965), *TV Guide's* critic, as "number-one actor of the year—the peerless Flipper."

Naturalists always have been as curious about whales as

ordinary people are. They have made observations at sea, but sometimes they had to wait to examine parts of whales' bodies until they were brought home by commercial whalers. Some of these parts were brought back as trophies: a jaw bone, a sperm whale tooth, a vertebra, parts of the ear—and these were often carved to while away the time on the long journeys. Anthony van Leeuwenhoek, who in the seventeenth century first discovered the microscopic world through his carefully ground lenses, felt himself lucky to be able to study a whale's eye, pickled in brandy, that was brought to him by a whaling ship's captain. And more than a century later, John Hunter, the great English anatomist and collector, tried to reconstruct the Leviathan from such parts as he could collect from his explorer friends. But the "collections" were too often disappointing: a young ship's surgeon, whom he had instructed to bring back preserved parts, handed him a shriveled piece of whale skin covered with parasites!

After years of using "whalebone" for corset stays, crinoline skirts, umbrellas, clock-springs, whips, sled-runners, and visors for hats, it was discovered that whalebone was not bone at all! The stiff but flexible substance, called baleen, taken from the upper jaw of certain whales, is actually horny material derived from the skin of the mouth, just as your nails are formed from

Sperm whale (*Physeter catodon*)

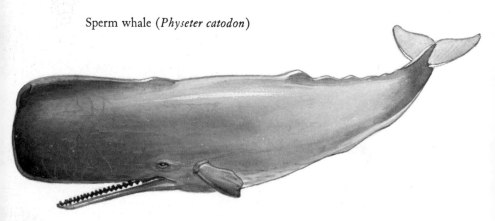

skin cells. (By a turn in economic history, this once-precious cargo, for which so many men lost their lives, is today one of the very few parts of the whale that are thrown overboard. Perhaps a new use for it will some day be found. The sperm whale, long ago hunted with hand harpoons from small boats, has a waxy *spermaceti* in a case in its head, at one time used to make candles. But its function in the living whale is still not fully understood.

There are many things that remain to be discovered about these mammals. Dolphins, the smaller members of this family, are being studied by specialists of every sort in various parts of the world. Dolphins were chosen for this intensive research because they can be transported to a tank laboratory on land.

Of course the capture and transportation—even of dolphins—was not easy; it took a number of failures and dogged persistence to do it successfully. And then ways had to be found of keeping them alive in captivity.

Netting and capturing

In the United States, the pioneer in getting dolphins to live in captivity was Dr. Charles H. Townsend, curator of the New York Aquarium when it was at Battery Park, at the southern tip of Manhattan. Back in 1912 he made his first attempt to put dolphins in a pool. They were sent to him from Pamlico Sound, North Carolina. Dr. Townsend had given careful instructions that the animals be kept cool and buoyed up in salt water, but his instructions were not heeded and the dolphins died on the way because they were shipped dry. After a third try, in 1913, he personally supervised the netting and transporting and succeeded in bringing back alive several porpoises. But with all the care they received, and despite Dr. Townsend's extensive knowledge of whales, the dolphins died, one by one, until the last was gone in less than two years.

The capturing of dolphins and the smaller whales is still a whale of a job. At first a strong twine net was laid around the sought-after captive and gradually drawn in, but the animal would detect its confining mesh and attempt to escape. Sometimes the struggle ended up in its getting completely entangled and, frightened, it would either stay motionless, or it would smash against the net. The struggle would often end in the animal's drowning in the very waters where it previously lived freely. If captured successfully, it then had to be shipped to its land destination. In the air, its delicate skin would become damaged by drying; when placed in a box-like tank with enough water to keep its body moist, it still sometimes bruised its skin or hurt its head or rib cage. If care was not taken to cool it with fresh salt water, it would become overheated.

As recently as 1962, when Captain William G. Gray, Director of Collections and Exhibits at the Miami Seaquarium, sought to capture the great prize Snowball—the only albino dolphin ever to have been kept in captivity (until she died in May 1965)—it took 22 days of hunting to capture it. Captain Gray described the final triumphant step in these words:

* * *

Above: Snowball, a Bottlenose dolphin (*Tursiops truncatus*); Right: Transporting a dolphin in a moistened, rubber, foam-lined sling

Just as he [Captain Hanson, his assistant in the venture] was about to close the net he had noticed a dozen or more large porpoises had come to the surface within the circle. Realizing that if so many porpoises became entangled in our net we might only have a slim chance of capturing the only two we wanted alive, we retrieved the net and made ready to start all over again. Some hours later we found her again in the same area and followed in readiness until she with her baby split off from the herd. This time we circled the pair successfully. At this point we anchored the mother ship and from two small boats began to tighten the circle of net. When Snowball realized the net was closing in she charged full speed and struck it . . . We lost no time in getting to her and rolling her into the boat. We delivered her promptly aboard the mother ship and placed her tied down on a sponge rubber mattress. Then we hastened back to the net where the baby was still struggling to get free. We rescued the baby and hurried back to place the baby alongside his mother. It was a boy.

After capturing a dolphin, and transporting it safely in a moistened sling lined with rubber foam, there is then the problem of getting it to live in captivity. Usually, it is first tempted with repeated offerings of live fish; later it is taught to eat dead fish.

While many problems of keeping dolphins healthy in captivity have been solved to some extent in the Marinelands of Florida and California, in the Seaquarium in Miami, and in research centers at Sea World Oceanarium in San Diego, Point Mugu Marine Biological Station, and Sea Life Park in Hawaii, a great deal of attention still has to be given to their environment.

One of Dr. Townsend's problems in 1912, for example, was the water, piped in from New York harbor; it was perhaps not as salty as it is in the ocean, and also it was probably contaminated, as harbor waters often are. (This problem of low salinity was thought also to be the reason for Moby Doll's illness and death in Vancouver. During its brief stay, Moby Doll had contracted, among other things, a fungus infection that turned its natural black, glossy skin to a dull gray.)

In the New York Aquarium, the tank water in which two

beluga whales are presently thriving is constantly renewed, 450 gallons of sea water flowing in per minute; thus cleansed and kept at 53 degrees the year round, the water is then passed through special biofilters. Two acres of stone surface covered with bacteria constitute these filters that keep the water purified and free from harmful substances.

When the problems of capturing small whales and raising them in captivity were largely solved, scientists felt ready to do experiments—in their accustomed way. But then they discovered that a dolphin cannot safely be given an anesthetic! As soon as it "goes under," not only its body movement, but everything else, stops—its breathing, and its heartbeat. (The problem of anesthesia gives promise of being solved in experienced hands, as you will read later.)

All of these problems are due to the fact that the whale family is so beautifully adapted to its watery home that by its very nature it resists being separated from it. Yet they are air-breathing animals whose early ancestors once lived on land! What makes the cetaceans unique is that they made the trip in evolution in *both* directions: from the ocean to the land—and back again.

In the last three or four decades, since scientists have been studying dolphins intensively, more questions have been raised than answers found. Nevertheless, the research continues.

Physicists are investigating the ability of whales to produce sounds and locate echoes, and psychologists are trying to find out how well they can learn, and how they communicate with each other. Physiologists are probing their large brains, and nutritionists wonder about how a 100-ton whale converts into flesh the tiny animals it scoops up from the ocean. Navy scientists hope to find the secret of the whale's seemingly effortless, streamlined motion that perhaps could show them how to improve the efficiency of surface ships and submarines. Other scientists are trying to understand the whale's built-in sonar system. Some have said it operates more effectively than any system yet devised by man to guide him through the ocean's deeps, but then they cannot really be compared: man's sonar can scan for miles, while the porpoise uses its only for close targets.

Will man some day be able to put cetaceans to work for him, as he has dogs and horses? Well, there is Tuffy, a dolphin trained for active service in the U.S. Navy's project Sealab II. Tuffy got his nickname by giving his trainers a hard time during his early days in a West Coast oceanarium after his capture in 1962. Also, he was and still is tough with sharks, and has many scars to prove it. Today this 10-year-old, 7-foot, 270-pound Atlantic bottlenose is domesticated, recently passing a test as aid to Sealab's aquanauts after a year's special training at the Point Mugu Naval Missile Center, California.

Tuffy wears a harness, and carries messages, mail, and needed supplies—such as drugs—from the surface to the divers living in the steel-cylinder laboratory, 210 feet down. But can he guide a lost diver safely back to base? He can, and he's done it. Carrying a strong nylon rope attached to his harness, he has come to the rescue of a diver signaling a distress "call" with a Strobe light and its audible on-and-off clicks, or one with simply a battery-powered buzzer. Tuffy has picked up clicks and buzzes at a distance of a third of a mile, reaching the "stranded" diver in a few minutes, and hauling him back to safety. Should a shark appear, call Tuffy!

Who can say in what other ways dolphins and other cetaceans may help people in the years ahead?

2

Early Ancestors and Living Relatives

ALL WHALES, both large and small, are known by the "family name" of *Cetacea*. In scientific classification the cetaceans are really not a family but an Order—a group next larger than a Family and next smaller than a Class. By the same system of naming living things, men and apes belong to the Order of Primates, and mice and muskrats to the Order of Rodents.

Two groups of water mammals that some people mistake for whale relatives are the *Pinnipeds*, and the Order of *Sirenians*. Seals, sea lions, and walruses are *pinnipeds*, so named because of their fin-like feet. Among the *sirenians*, which are plant-eating water mammals, are the dugong and manatee, or sea cow. These rather unprepossessing, even ugly (to us) creatures, must have been named by highly imaginative and homesick sailors in ancient times, for Greek mythology says that a siren was a sea nymph having the head and body of a woman and the tail of a bird. By their enticing singing, sirens were supposed to have lured sailors to their deaths on rocky coasts.

Neither the *pinnipeds* nor *sirenians* are in the whale family. In 400 B.C., twenty-three centuries before biologists divided plants and animals into orders and families and gave them their present Latin names, Aristotle grouped whales, porpoises, and dolphins together as they still are—cetaceans—placing them high on his "ladder of life." Strange it is, therefore, that up to about two centuries ago people continued to believe that whales were fish. They "have a blowhole and are provided with lungs and breathe," Aristotle said, and they are "provided with milk and suckle their young."

25

If you wonder how animals of such diverse size can be in the same group, remember that the Great Dane and the Chihuahua are both dogs. It is not known exactly how the cetaceans got their name, but the Latin *cetus* (the Greek *ketos*), meaning "large sea animal," was happily chosen for the sixty or more whale cousins. Whatever their individual differences, they are large, air-breathing mammals, almost entirely hairless, and completely aquatic. No other animals have all these characteristics.

Not until the eighteenth century did scientists once and for all classify whales as mammals—animals whose young are born alive and brought up on the mother's milk. A whale or a porpoise is no more a fish than you or I, and is more closely related to man than to fishes. That it lives in water does not change the overriding fact that like you and me it breathes air and has lungs, while fish extract dissolved oxygen from the water that passes over their gills.

According to where they live, animals may be divided (not according to scientific classification) into three kinds: aquatic or water inhabitants, terrestrial or land-living, and amphibious— those that live both in water and on land. Living wholly in water as fish do, and living only on land as most birds and mammals do, are very different modes of life. And those which, so to say, have one foot in the water and the other on land, such as frogs and salamanders (true amphibians), live still another kind of life.

Very different structures are required for water living and land living. For example, as a very minimum, true aquatic animals must be able to get oxygen from the water, and their body structure must be specially suited to swimming and diving but not to getting around on land; terrestrial (land-living) animals must have lungs for getting oxygen from the air, and limbs adapted for walking, crawling, leaping, or flying.

Whatever its present habitat, every animal is descended from earlier water forms, because all of the first animals to appear on our planet lived in the sea. At that time the land itself was very different from what it is now; there were no plants on the land and so it could not support life. To see how it all began we would have to turn the earth's calendar back an estimated half billion years, but this is another story and would take us too far away from our whales. However, scientists have found a great deal of evidence to prove that just as the earth constantly changed—and is still changing—so animals also changed slowly and gradually. With passing generations, these small, step-like changes, over millions and millions of years, piled up into big changes. At certain periods in the history of the earth, such big changes resulted in the appearance of ever new kinds of living beings: first the many soft-bodied animals without backbones; then those with backbones: fishes, amphibians, reptiles (the first land animals), birds, and mammals, including man.

At various times during the long parade, sea animals left the water and took up life on dry land. This invasion of the land followed changes in the earth's surface and climate. Mountains were heaved up by giant foldings of the earth's crust; the seas receded, rivers dried up in some places, and elsewhere the land became submerged under spreading waters. To make a successful move from water to land, animals had to be equipped with appropriate body parts for breathing, feeding, and getting about on land. If a sudden dry period occurred, those not equipped to make the transition to a land existence died out— became extinct. Some that were in a halfway stage of adaptation to land must have kept close to the water's edge, spending part of their time in water and part on land. Only those that were best suited to life on land could succeed in the competition for food, win the battle with natural enemies, and increase their numbers—until a new change threatened their continued existence. For instance, the cumbersome, sluggish dinosaurs (ancient reptiles) gave way to the first mammals—small but fleet, warm-blooded, furry animals with better-developed brains and sense organs. When the jungle swamps dried up, the lush ferns withered and died, and a cold period set in, the huge dinosaurs were at a disadvantage, while the much smaller mammals were well equipped for the change. Being neither nimble nor brainy, the dinosaurs lost out in the battle for food, and were doomed to extinction.

Describing the extinction of a great many reptiles about 125 million years ago, one biologist writes:

. . . they were apparently unable to adapt to the marked changes brought about by the Rocky Mountain Revolution. As the climate became colder and drier many of the plants which served as food for the herbivorous reptiles disappeared. Some of the herbivorous reptiles were too large to walk about on land when the swamps dried up. The smaller, warm-blooded mammals which had appeared were better able to compete for food and many of them ate reptilian eggs. The demise of the many kinds of reptiles was probably the result of a combination of a whole host of factors, rather than any single one.

While, in general, the forward march seemed to have been onto the land, with birds and mammals most independent of their ancestral home, many animals at some time returned, either partially or wholly, to the water. The biologist offers some possible explanations.

As the number of animals on land increased, the available food diminished, while in the sea food was abundant. Those animals whose structure and habits did not completely separate them from aquatic life were able to take to the water for food, and incidentally for refuge from enemies that were not as well equipped for life in the water. Others were water-bound by their breeding habits—the need to lay their eggs in shallow quiet streams. Frogs, for instance, must deposit their eggs in water to protect them from drying out.

Frogs and salamanders are not the only ones to lead a double life. Many mammals also straddle the water's edge. To mention only a few: water shrews and fishing rats scurry to the water to feed on fish; muskrats and beavers feed on frogs and fish as well as on water grasses. And not only rodents, but the otter, a relative of the mink and weasel and an excellent swimmer and diver, feeds chiefly on fish. Although the otter also eats snails, slugs, earthworms, rats, and birds, it is admirably adapted to life in the water. Its nostrils and ears can be closed, keeping water out when it is submerged; its webbed toes make swimming easier and less tiring over long distances; its sleek body narrows imperceptibly into its thick tail—a streamlined feature for swift getaway in the water.

In the return to aquatic life, some animals stayed close to shore, others made longer excursions, and still others almost completely separated themselves from the land. A living example of the last kind is the seal. Very much at home in water, still it comes out on shore for a sunning, it breathes air, and it *must* return to land to mate and have its young. But while seals can haul themselves out onto beaches or rocks, they do not get about as easily on land as they do in water, not doing as well as sea lions, which use all four limbs to move on the ground. On the other hand, the true seals need hardly raise their heads to breathe in water because their nostrils are almost on top of the head, while sea lions' nostrils are at the tip of the snout and they have to raise their heads to breathe.

Even so, seals are not as fully prepared as whales for aquatic life. Not only must the cow return to land to mate with the bull and to give birth; it also has to train the newborn seal pup to swim. But whales complete their life cycle without ever having to leave the water. In fact, they cannot survive when beached (stranded on land). Also, their young do not have to be taught to swim, although the baby whale may need a free ride on its mother's back to keep up with fast-swimming schools. Another important feature that distinguishes these two animals is the hairlessness of the whale. All other mammals have fur, hair, or a woolly coat. This cover, like a blanket, does prevent excessive cooling of the body, but it also has its disadvantages. Take, for example, the harp seals, born on ice floes: if one accidentally falls into the water before its thick, woolly birth coat is lost, it has trouble staying afloat because the fur becomes waterlogged. Whales are born hairless, and except for a few bristles on the snout in some species and in others around the blowhole, they never grow either body hair or fur.

If whales are so well adapted to marine life, how is it biologists tell us that their distant ancestors were landlubbers? As proof they have reconstructed, from hundreds of clues, a story of gradual changeover from a four-legged land animal to the aquatic form. As is not uncommon in the sciences, some links in the chain of events are missing, and with more knowledge certain details may have to be altered. But in its main outlines the story is built on the kind of evidence the biologist has accumulated for the evolution of other living things. Picking up clues one after another and fitting them into a believable story, a detective can track down a crime that no one ever witnessed; in much the same way scientists build the story of evolution on "circumstantial evidence." Let's examine the evidence in the strange case of the whale's ancestry.

Some clues are to be found in the body of the modern whale itself and in the developing whale embryo; others have been discovered in the earth's rock layers, where skeletal remains point to earlier land forms.

When we look at the long slender body of a whale making its way so easily and gracefully through the water, it reminds us more of a submarine seen in an underwater movie than of a four-legged mammal. In fact, it has no legs at all, and the two small fin-like flippers it has in front would do it no good at all on land. It propels its body through the water with its powerful tail, which it moves up and down much as the frog-man uses his flippers. But while the frog-man works his legs alternately, the dolphin moves its double-fluked tail as one piece from its attachment to the body. The fluke, once thought to be a fusion of the whale's hind limbs, is now known to have no bones; it is an extension of the skin and fibrous tissue of the tail.

Not only have its hind legs disappeared but also its outer ears, and there is no external evidence of a nose or other mammalian protuberances such as the milk glands and the external genitals. Thus the whale's body is streamlined for fast, easy, and unrestricted motion, with the flippers used mostly for steering and for controlling diving angle and trim. If we were to judge only from these superficial features, we would find nothing that resembles any land mammal with which we are familiar. So the biologist has to search for clues in hidden parts of the cetacean anatomy.

When the massive muscles in the whale are cut away on both sides, just a little in front of the anal opening, a slender bone about 12 inches long is discovered, with sometimes a stump of another bone extending from it. The long one, no longer attached to the lower portion of the spine as it is in land mammals, is a remnant of what was once a hip bone. It is completely useless to the whale for locomotion but, in the male, it serves as an attachment for muscles related to the movement of the penis. Another occasional bony stump is a vestige of the femur, or thigh bone. Just as its outer ears have disappeared from view, so its hind limbs have shriveled away from lack of use. The outer ear in land mammals serves to collect the sound waves, making hearing easier; the whale has no use for this aid, since sound travels faster and with less displacement in water. But the muscles that moved it are still there beneath the skin, and this is taken as proof that whales once had external ears.

The next clue is in the flipper. Dissected to the bone, it reveals a more visible link to land mammals because much more has remained of the forelimbs than of the hind ones. All the bones that make up the arm in man are there, even though proportionately smaller and otherwise modified. The upper arm bone (*humerus*) and those of the forearm (*radius* and *ulna*) are

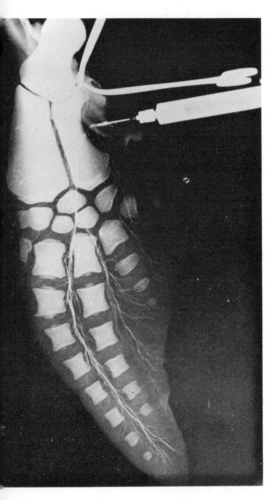

X-ray of flipper, showing bones resembling "wrist" and "hand" of land animals. Hypodermic needle is in position to draw blood sample from artery

much foreshortened and also flattened. With the exception of one group of whales, the rorquals, all cetaceans have five "fingers," as well as "wrist" and "hand" bones. And so, hidden in the fleshy mitten of the flipper, we find evidence of a forelimb that once must have had another use.

The other bony parts of the whale—the skull, spinal column and rib cage—resemble those of other mammals. Where there are differences—and there are many—they have a bearing on the whale's superb swimming ability. For example, whales and many dolphins have practically no neck, with little narrowing between the body and the head. Yet the backbone shows the same seven neck bones that other mammals have, whether the neck is as long as the giraffe's or as short as the sea otter's. In some dolphins and the larger whales these bones are actually fused and no longer movable—another modification for aquatic life. So also the skull tapers into the pointed snout, and the blowhole has shifted up and back into the forehead. When you read later

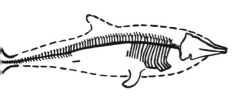

Vertebral column of Common dolphin and of dog

about other skeletal features and the internal organs, you will see the clear resemblance of whales to cows, horses, and men; but the special changes demanded for life in the water are always striking.

Further proof that the whale had a land ancestor is furnished by the embryologist. In the very young embryo (about an inch long) there are rudimentary hind limbs resembling those of other mammals, and these embryonic limbs betray a once terrestrial existence. In older embryos these limbs have become flattened to nothing but traces. (Recently a porpoise with two protruding hind limbs was caught off the coast of Japan.) The fluke, on the contrary, is absent in the very early stages and shows up only later in the development of the embryo. Perhaps a small detail, but full of meaning in the whale's evolution, is the presence of hair in the fetus, located near the blowhole-to-be and the eyes. The later "baldness" of the fully formed whale is part of its wonderful equipment for fast swimming.

Tracing the family tree of the cetaceans to their nearest ancestors, scientists point to fossils in the earth's layers. The soft parts of any prehistoric animal have long disappeared, but from the preserved skeletal remains the appearance of the living animal may be reconstructed. In North America, Europe, New Zealand, and in the Antarctic, fossils have been found of animals estimated to have lived some 35 million years ago. Some of these skeletons are snake-shaped and others are closer in shape to modern whales. All of them seem to have had smaller flukes and seven separate and movable vertebrae in the neck; their fin-shaped limbs are believed to have been movable at the elbow; the hip bones had sockets for the ball-shaped head of the thigh bones, as well as a large opening for nerves and blood vessels present in the pelvic bones of land mammals.

These ancestral cetaceans, which became extinct about 25 million years ago, had other characteristics that link them to modern whales. The position of the nostrils was more nearly like that of the horse or dog—at the tip of the snout—and in the very young embryos of modern cetaceans the nostrils are still in this position; only later in their development does the blowhole migrate to its typical position at the top of the head. When your dog swims, he assumes, in order to breathe, an oblique position with his head upward, allowing the nostrils to be out of water. When the whale is swimming, its body is almost horizontal, the snout submerged, but its blowhole is above the surface.

Aristotle, the careful Greek observer, watched the dolphin "asleep with his nose above water, and snoring." He noted that through its blowhole it inhales air into its lungs, "so that if caught in a net [under water] he is quickly suffocated for lack of air."

The fossil skeletons found in several parts of the world something over a century ago belonged to animals called *Archaeocetes*, meaning old or primitive cetaceans. A reconstructed *Archaeocete* skeleton discovered in Alabama is on exhibit at the National Museum in Washington. Since it is more like a terrestrial mammal than a modern cetacean, it is believed to be one link in the chain that connects modern whales with their dry land ancestors. Scientists believe that there was probably more than one branch from which our whales came because two distinct suborders of cetaceans exist today. At any rate, these fossil remains, along with the clues in the whale's anatomy, both embryonic and fully developed, provide some of the evidence for its pedigree.

Although it is pretty certain that ancestral whales did indeed exchange their home on land for one in the water, the reason for this turnabout is not known. But according to Dr. Roy Chapman Andrews, explorer and naturalist, one thing is sure: the giants in the family could not have reached their present size if they had remained on land, for the size of land animals is limited by the weight their legs will support. The bulky dinosaurs could move only very slowly and with a lumbering gait. In water, animals do not depend on the support of limbs because they are buoyed up by the water—especially salt water—which reduces the pull of gravity that land animals have to contend with. And so, unlike land animals, whales can grow to their enormous size without collapsing under their own weight.

There are two suborders of cetacea: the *Mystacoceti* (also *Mysticeti* or *Mysticetes*) which get their name from the Greek word *mysta* meaning mustache; and the *Odontoceti* or toothed whales. If you like, you can forget these scientific names and simply remember that they stand for the two major groups: those that have the enormous plates and mat-like sieve in their mouths made of a material called baleen or "whalebone"; and those that have teeth. Dolphins and porpoises, the smaller cousins, are toothed whales. The only large toothed whale is the sperm whale of Moby Dick fame. The two groups are chiefly distinguished by their food and feeding habits. But related to this are differences in structure of the jaw and mouth, body size, migrations in search of food, and the depths to which the animals dive for it. The baleen whales have no use for teeth because their diet consists of plankton, especially small shrimp. Plankton, the Greek word for "that which drifts," consists of billions of plants and animals of all shapes and sizes floating on and near the ocean's surface. With the help of its tongue and that remarkable horny structure—the baleen plates and bristle curtains—the whale strains out its food from the sea water.

The toothed whales have a row of peg-like teeth, some only

in the lower jaw, which are not used for chewing but only for snatching and holding on to slippery fish which are swallowed whole. (See picture on page 41.) The sperm whale, with teeth shaped the same as the dolphin's but larger, eats mainly cuttle-fish, including the giant squid. Other differences are the wide jawbones and double blowholes of the baleen whales, and the not so wide jaws and single blowhole of the toothed whales.

There are several families of baleen whales. You will find their scientific names in the table at the end of this book, but most people call them by their common names. Some have dor-sal fins and some are finless; some have long whalebone and no grooves on the throat, while others have short baleen and throat grooves. Let's meet the more important ones—important mainly because they are better known, but not always for commercial reasons.

The names of different whales are often descriptive of some special feature, but it is not always clear how some of them got their names. Take the right whales, for example. An old-time whaler would have told you that these whales were the "right" ones to hunt. What he meant is that a right whale is a slow swimmer, can more easily be harpooned, does not sink when killed, and has the "right" amount of oil. We now know that proportionately they have a large quantity of fat, so that their carcasses *do* float. And because they are not fast swimmers it was easier for the early whalers, equipped only with hand har-poons and small boats, to go after them, and they practically killed them off. There are three kinds, the Greenland right whale, about 50 feet long, once abundant in the Arctic Ocean, and found also in the Pacific (Okhotsk Sea and Bering Sea); the Pigmy right whale, in the Antarctic; and the Biscayan right whale, hunted by the Basques as early as the thirteenth century. The Biscayan right whale is of three types or subspecies: the North Atlantic, North Pacific, and Southern hemisphere. It ranges widely over the Atlantic, and it has recently been ob-

Greenland right whale (*Balaena mysticetus*)

served in tropical seas. The Greenland whale, also known as the bowhead because of its enormous arched head, has whalebone plates as long as 14 feet. It had been hunted almost to extinction, and those that remain are now jealously protected by international law; as a result their number is increasing.

The 40-to-45-foot-long California gray whale that once was abundant in the North Pacific was hunted so intensely that it disappeared off the California coast for decades (roughly 1870 to 1920) and then turned up off the coast of Japan, where in 1912 it was "rediscovered" by Roy Chapman Andrews. Two complete skeletons of this whale were assembled by him and may be seen in the United States—one in the American Museum of Natural History in New York, the other in the Smithsonian Institution in Washington. Now that measures have been taken to conserve them, they are returning to the eastern Pacific, each year in greater numbers. In the past few years several thousand have been seen during their migration to the lagoons of Baja California, along the coast of Sinaloa, Mexico where they go to breed between November and February. With the renewed interest in whales, thousands of tourists go out on excursion boats to view the awesome southerly parade of these California gray whales.

The bodies of the so-called right whales, except for the rare pigmy right whale, are thick and relatively short—only about 50 feet! They have enormous bowed heads, no dorsal fin (the

California gray has a number of knobs where the dorsal fin would be), and their flippers are short, broad, and paddle-shaped. They show no throat or belly folds or grooves. (Because of these modifications in structure it is usually classified as a separate species, intermediate between the right whales and the rorquals.) Slow swimmers, they also do not dive as far down as the fin whales.

As the name tells us, the fin whales or rorquals (meaning fin) have a dorsal fin. What distinguishes them most, however, is their size, for among the fins we find the true giants: the blue whales, sometimes called "sulphurbottoms" (because of the yellow film on the sides and bellies due to microscopic plants that live harmlessly on them), and the fin whales or finbacks. The blue whale is about twice as long (100 feet or more) as the average right whale, and the fin whale grows as long as 70 feet.

The rorqual has a long, slender body, the head is not arched but flat and somewhat triangular, as in fish, and its baleen is comparatively short—three to four feet long. They have parallel grooved folds, like pleats, on the throat and belly, a feature which may serve to increase the throat capacity when the whale opens its mouth to scoop up food. It has also been suggested that they help in cooling the whale. The dorsal fin at about the hind third of the body, is a boneless projection of skin and blubber which probably helps in balancing.

Highly streamlined, these whales are fast swimmers, which is one reason why they escaped the earlier whale hunters. Also, their huge bulk was not so vulnerable to the hand harpoon; moreover the harpoon could not be thrust with any accuracy without getting very close to the prey, and it was no small risk for a small boat to get next to an 80- or 90-foot whale. As likely as not the boat would be smashed into splinters with one flail of the giant's fluke. It was only when whalers went out on fast steamships, equipped with harpoon guns and bomb lances that exploded in the body of the whale a few minutes after they were fired, that the rorquals became the more recent over-hunted

Throat grooves and underside of flipper of Blue whale

whale victims. They do not float when killed, either, and so to
prevent the carcass's sinking it had to be pumped up with air,
if the hunter was not to lose his catch. In sounding (diving),
they reach much greater depths than the right whales, and
sometimes surface again half a mile away.

Fin whales feed on small shrimp from about half an inch
to three inches long, so while the blue whale and finback are
found in all waters, they are more numerous in the Antarctic
where this particular shrimp practically covers the sea. It is here
in the Antarctic that most are hunted today, but they are also
caught in the North Atlantic and West Pacific.

Four other kinds of fin whales are the sei, little piked or
Minke whale (named for Meincke, a whaler, who was supposed
to have mistaken a herd of piked whales for blue whales; whalers poked fun at him by referring to the "dwarf" among whales
as Minke), Bryde's whale, and the humpback. Except for the
humpback, all fin whales have the same sleek, streamlined bodies and graceful motion. The little piked whale, up to 30 feet
long, is hunted in the North Atlantic and off Japan. Bryde's
whale is the only rorqual found entirely in tropical waters; the
sei whale, slimmer and smaller than the fin whale, is especially
known for its fast swimming.

The humpback, about 45 feet long, is distinguished by un-
sightly knobs on the top of its head and on its chin and jaws,
and by the humplike dorsal fin. Its flippers are immense, some
15 feet long, and they are covered with barnacles, the kind
found on ships' bottoms and piers. Barnacles attach themselves
to the humpback's chin and throat.

The toothed whales comprise many more families than the
baleens. The best known is the sperm whale, of which there are
two kinds: the large *Physeter catodon,* hunted intensively from
the eighteenth to about the middle of the nineteenth century,
and still taken by the thousands, particularly off Japan; and
the Pigmy. Both are found in all seas. The large one has enor-

Baby Sperm whale, about four or five months old when captured, showing teeth in lower jaw. (The whale lived only a few days at the Miami Seaquarium)

mous teeth in its lower jaw; the teeth in its upper jaw, which extends beyond the lower, are less prominent, some being hidden in the gum. Its head, nearly half the length of its body, is box-like, almost square. The blowhole is on the left side of its head. This asymmetry is thought to have occurred in its ancestors: as the large spermaceti case developed and filled with light, wax-like oil, the nostrils were pushed off center and so shifted to their present position. This lack of symmetry is also found in other *odontocetes*. For example, the nasal partition is tilted in both the narwhal and bottlenose whale. (*Odontocetes* in general have many asymmetries in the upper front end of the skull.)

Dall's porpoise (*Phocoenoides dalli*)

The male sperm whale is considerably larger than the female, measuring up to 60 feet compared with the female's 38 feet. This difference is marked enough so that usually a bull can be differentiated from a cow in the open sea. They are gray, but albinos are known to exist; Melville's Moby Dick, though a sperm whale, was a great white whale.

While some toothed whales, such as the Pacific killer, reach a length of 30 feet, and the pilot whales reach up to 20 feet, most of the other families consist of dolphins and porpoises, ranging in length from about 3 to 8 feet. Some dolphins live in rivers—the susu or Gangetic dolphin in the Ganges and Indus rivers, and the boutu in the Amazon—but most of them live in the ocean. None except the beaked whales (with two grooves) have grooves in the throat. Their tails are notched, as a rule, and usually they have teeth in both upper and lower jaws. Exceptions are Dall's porpoise and some beaked whales with one or two needle-like remnants of teeth.

Here we come to a confusion of names. This doesn't seem to bother the experts, but it is troublesome to those of us who find out that the pilot whale, the beluga or white whale, and the narwhal are all really dolphins! Because of their larger size, they are called whales, but scientists classify them as *Delphinidae,* in the "wider sense;" while the killer whale, larger than the other three, is classified under "dolphins in the stricter sense." Not only this, but dolphins are sometimes referred to as porpoises, especially in the United States, while the common porpoise of

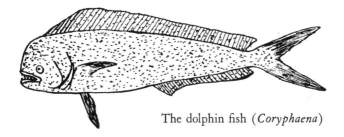

The dolphin fish (*Coryphaena*)

the North Atlantic, also called the harbor porpoise (*Phocoena phocoena*), is also placed in this conglomerate group of *Delphinidae sensu lato* ("dolphins in the wider sense").

Without even trying to unscramble the dolphin-porpoise naming system, we know one thing about the name, and it must be understood: there is a true fish called "dolphin." It is a large game fish with the scientific name *Coryphaena*, but known from the Western Pacific to the Caribbean Sea and in Hawaii as

Diver with Beluga whales (*Delphinapterus leucas*)

Spotted dolphin, or porpoise (*Stenella plagiodon*)

"mahi mahi." You can see from the picture on page 43 that it is not of the whale family. It breathes with gills, has the fins and tail of a fish, is in all other ways a real fish, and is prized for its excellent eating qualities.

As for the rest, here is what a dolphin expert, Captain William B. Gray of the Miami Seaquarium, has to say:

> The books on the Cetacea clan inform us that "those with beaks are called dolphins. The ones having a short snout are classed as porpoises." . . . But Dall's porpoise, which is common about the Aleutian Islands, and the white-beaked dolphins of most northern oceans are both commonly known as dolphins although they both display a very short stubby snout. The Irrauaddy [Irrawaddy] porpoise of the Asiatic coast has no snout at all . . . [And] the long-snouted dolphin commonly called "spotted porpoise" is often seen playing around the prows of ships at sea.

So the Captain's best answer, when asked "Which is proper, porpoise or dolphin?" is "If you refer to them unscientifically by either name I think anyone familiar with the creature will know what you mean."

According to another expert, Antony Alpers of New Zealand:

> In the United States dolphins of any kind are usually called porpoises, and the same thing tends to happen in New Zealand. To

me the name that comes from the Greek seems both more beautiful and more correct, and I prefer to use it, reserving "porpoise" as the English do for those slightly smaller members of the dolphin family that have no beak . . . and whose teeth are spade-shaped instead of conical.

While the name "dolphin" comes from the Greeks, "porpoise" comes from the French *porc-poisson,* meaning "pig-fish." The Roman naturalist Pliny thought that porpoises were gloomy-looking, lacking the playfulness of dolphins and having the evil look of dogfish. And so, expressing his greater fondness for dolphins, Alpers sums up: "Apart from all these differences, real and imagined dolphins and porpoises are virtually the same animal, for they both belong to the family of cetaceans known

Common dolphin (*Delphinus delphis*) being hand-fed

to zoologists as *Delphinidae,* and the *Delphinidae* in turn are *Odontoceti,* or toothed cetaceans."

Trying to avoid confusion for their readers in this matter of naming, scientists sometimes preface their reports by clarifying the particular definition they have adopted. For example, Mr. David H. Brown and Dr. Kenneth S. Norris introduce their observations in California's Marineland as follows:

We follow Norman and Fraser (1940) in their definition of the terms *porpoise* and *dolphin;* porpoise refers to members of the *Delphinidae* which are small, beakless, and with triangular dorsal fins and tricuspid teeth. *Dolphin* is used for the remainder of the family, except those larger forms dignified by the name *whale.*

The cetacean now receiving the most intensive study, and whose picture you are familiar with from magazines, movies, and television, is the bottlenose dolphin or *Tursiops truncatus* (see picture, page 21). *Tursiops* is Latin for porpoise and *truncatus* refers to its snubnosed snout that is said to resemble the opening of an old-fashioned bottle. (This is not the common dolphin *Delphinus delphis,* usually seen in schools accompanying ships and playfully leaping around their bows.)

Tursiops is naturally an inhabitant of generally temperate seas: the Atlantic, Pacific (off Japan, Hawaii), and the Red Sea. It also thrives in captivity in the warm waters of Florida, Southern California, and the Virgin Islands. It has a well-defined snout and a fairly high dorsal fin. Its color is gray, with a lighter gray-to-white throat and belly. When fully grown it weighs around 500 or 600 pounds and is about 8 feet long, but may reach a length of 13 feet. Both jaws contain teeth (a variable number of about 40 to 44 pairs) which interlock.

Another dolphin is the pilot whale, commonly called "blackfish," the male 20 feet long and the female 16 feet. It is nearly all black, with some lighter area on the belly; its bulbous forehead overhangs a short beak; its flippers are long and narrow, and each jaw has 8 to 10 pairs of teeth. It is found in the

Bimbo, Pacific Pilot whale
(*Globicephala scammoni*),
Capt. William Gray (above)

North Atlantic Pilot whale showing characteristic
white markings and long flippers

Pacific, from the Gulf of California to Alaska, traveling in schools, or pods, numbering hundreds, and feeding on small fish or squid. In Newfoundland and the Faroe Islands, North Atlantic pilot whales (a different species from the Pacific pilot whale) are driven into shallow bays where it is simpler to obtain their oil and meat. (They can adapt to life in captivity; these whales have been trained in the "school" at Marineland of the Pacific and of Florida and regularly perform for spectators there, and in other oceanaria in California and Japan.)

Pilot whales are sometimes confused with the Pacific killer whale, but the two are quite different. While the killer is black, it has distinctive white markings behind the eye, a saddle-shaped area on the belly and under the flukes and flipper. Also, its dorsal fin is sharp, high, and triangular-shaped in the male, and hooked in the female; its snout is pointed rather than bulbous as in the pilot whale; each jaw carries 10 to 14 pairs of strong interlocking teeth; and, despite its name, it is at home in all oceans. The largest male found on the west coast of North America measured 22 feet, and the largest female 19 feet, but in other parts of the world it has been known to reach a length of 30 feet. The killer is the only whale that habitually preys upon other warm-blooded animals, including other whales.

Porpoises and dolphins have been hunted throughout the ages, their oil used for heating and lighting, and their meat for food. It is said that porpoise was once considered a great delicacy by English royalty, and that Henry VII had it served at his Coronation Dinner. Porpoises also provided food for the peoples of Normandy, Denmark, Norway, and the countries bordering on the Mediterranean and Black Seas.

Some species are easily caught because they swim close to shore in bays and fjords, traveling in pods in great numbers. They are caught in various ways: with nets and guns off the Black Sea coast; with knives, after being chased ashore in inlets of the Baltic Sea; on some South Pacific Islands, ancient magic is still used to lure the animals to the coast where the men surround them and by hand-clapping, shouting, and other noises drive them ashore.

Fresh-water dolphins are caught with nets, mostly for meat, in the large rivers of South America, India, and Tung Ting Lake in China. The oil of the Indian Gangetic dolphin is used for burning, and as a remedy for rheumatism. The boutu or Amazonian dolphin, on the other hand, is not killed for superstitious reasons and because, practically, it hunts the deadly and feared piranha. Because of its small eyes, it is believed to strike blind anyone who uses its oil in a lamp. It is also believed that during celebrations and ceremonial feasts the boutu comes ashore and joins in the festivities, and when it departs it leaves a child behind.

For whatever reasons, man still hunts members of the whale family. If you think that whaling ended with the romantic bygone days, remember that during the 1930–31 season 41 floating factories killed 28,325 blue whales—the most valuable prey of modern whalers—and 8,601 fin whales. To be sure, in the 1964–65 season the "fish" weren't "running," so that the 8,000 units (1 blue whale is a unit; 1 fin whale is $\frac{1}{2}$ unit) set as a quota by the Antarctic whaling nations—Norway, the Soviet Union, The Netherlands, and Japan—was barely fulfilled. And this was simply because, and in spite of quotas, these large whales are being killed at a faster rate than they can multiply.

Today, therefore, man must be concerned also with the conservation of whales. As Dr. E. J. Slijper, well-known Dutch whale researcher, has written: "Let us hope there will be whales in the sea, and whale-meat in our larders, as long as man continues on earth." To achieve this, increased knowledge of their structure, habits, behavior, and especially their remarkable adaptation to water, will play a major role. As a biologist, Dr. Slijper sees, in the study of whales, "at one and the same time the study of life on earth."

Two Blue whales (*Balaenoptera musculus*) and a Fin whale
(*Balaenoptera physalus*) being towed tail first behind a factory ship

3

Weighing a Whale

THE MOST STRIKING thing about the large whales is their enormous dimensions and bulk. They are so big, by the standards of living things, that a mere recital of their weights and measurements will not help you to visualize their mammoth size. This is why scientists, trying to describe them, often resort to comparisons with other "large" animals. Even experienced whalers and explorers are awed by the sight of a blue whale.

In your imagination, try to match a blue whale with the weight of 30 elephants, 3 Brontosauri, perhaps 100 head of cattle, or anything else that will add up to a weight of 150 tons (2,000 average-sized men). If you think an elephant is big, think of one standing up on the floor of a blue whale's open mouth without ever touching its upper jawbone!

Stranded whales have been measured: their length from the tip of the snout to the end of the fluke, the expanse of the flippers, the spread of the fluke, and the girth behind the flippers. When even a small stranded whale is brought to the attention of a museum curator, all its dimensions are faithfully recorded. Here's an example, from part of a record of a Baird's dolphin discovered by two youngsters on the beach at Victoria, B. C. and reported to *The Canadian Field-Naturalist* in 1954 by C. J. Guiguet of the Provincial Museum:

The animal was in an excellent state of preservation, so recently dead that no apparent decomposition had set in. The specimen bore many superficial scars but had succumbed rather quickly, it seemed, to a mechanical injury which was apparent at the base of the skull. The stomach was filled to capacity with digested herring.

51

The dolphin was an adult male weighing 119 pounds, with 86 teeth in each jaw. Among the measurements taken were the total length from tip to snout to hind margin of flukes—5 feet 10½ inches; from tip of snout to blowhole, 1 foot 1 inch; from the hind margin of the fluke to the anus, 1 foot 8 inches; the height of the dorsal fin was 6 inches; the length of the head was 1 foot 2½ inches; breadth of the body at the blowhole was 8½ inches; and so on to even the half-inch thickness of the blubber on the flank in line with the dorsal fin.

Try to picture the length of a blue whale: 100 feet. How long is 100 feet? The distance between the bases on a baseball diamond is 90 feet; the length of a tennis court is 78 feet; and an average-size swimming pool is 75 feet long. A full-grown blue whale would not fit into such a pool! And how would you picture 150 tons? You may have seen road signs warning about a bridge ahead: "Truckload limit 5 tons" or "Maximum load 15 tons." About the heaviest load a trailer-truck can carry is 15 tons. If even a fair-sized whale could be laid across such a bridge, the bridge would collapse.

And how would you weigh such a whale? Even if you could lift the weight of 13 cattle trucks—a comparison made by one whale expert—where would you get the scale? Think of only the jawbone and the fins, which in one blue whale weighed 5,000 pounds and 2,000 pounds respectively, and you have an idea of what it means to weigh a whale, and why until about 40 years ago whale weights were only rough estimates—a ton for a foot of body length—estimates that have since been revised as scientists have learned how to actually weigh them.

Before whaling ships were equipped with modern power machinery, making it possible to haul an entire carcass up a skidway or slipway and onto the deck, whale-weighing was practically impossible. Until the 1920's, flensing or peeling off of the blubber was done outboard. A good portion of the carcass

Shore station whaling. Hauling out (above); Flensing (below)
(From a mural in the Chicago Natural History Museum)

was discarded before it reached the ship, so that even if whalers were interested in weighing the catch (and they weren't) the result would not have been accurate.

The giant, machine-powered steel claw that lifts the whale onto a modern factory ship not only has eliminated this waste but incidentally has allowed the weighing of an entire animal almost as accurately as if it were placed intact on a scale—that is, piece by piece as it is stripped, hacked, and sawed up for dispatching the body sections to the appropriate boilers, bins, and barrels. This gross weight, of course, is not what the scientist most wants to know. He is interested mainly in the relative weights of the separate organs and tissues—muscles, bone, heart, blood. In this sense, carcasses are not often weighed because whalers ordinarily have no time for the laborious and time-consuming task of separating out each part.

As of yore, the first law in whale catching is not to hold up the processing of the carcass. So, except for scientists who go along on whaling ships and have studied whale anatomy, there is still no time to learn about the captive, even on the deck of a modern floating whale factory. Here the flenser strips the whale of its thick blubber, the lemmer cuts the meat, and the skeleton is sawed apart. Within a few hours, all that remains of the colossal catch are tanks of oil of different grades, pulverized "meal" from its meat and bones, vitamin-A-rich liver oil, and literally mountains of meat that will find its way to family tables in Norway, Japan, England, the Soviet Union, Chile, and Peru. You can also find it on the menus of the most expensive New York restaurants. And, believe it or not, among the later manufactured products are margarine, cold cream, lipstick, stains and varnishes, lubricants for airplane and submarine engines, poultry feed, cattle fodder, fertilizer for the soil, tinned food for pets, and precious hormones used in medicine, extracted from the whale's pituitary, pancreas, thyroid, and other glands.

It is easy to see, therefore, that in the highly organized processing of a whale there is little interest in the meticulous job that such a dissection requires. This is why Dr. E. J. Slijper was astonished when he learned that as many as 46 whales of different kinds had been weighed, one way or another, at the time he was writing his book on the biology of cetaceans, first published in 1958. And at that, most of this work had been done at land stations where the men don't have to work at the speed and split-second timing necessary on board ship.

Doctor Slijper wrote that, as of 1950, the weight record of 134 long tons was held by a 90-foot blue whale. (A *long* ton, the weight unit commonly used in Great Britain, continental Europe and other parts of the world,* is 2,240 pounds, while the *short* ton, used in the United States and Canada, is 2,000 pounds. So this whale weighed 150 short tons.) In one of the "Discovery Reports" (*Discovery* is the name of a British whale research ship), Alec H. Laurie, a British physiologist, gives the weight of a 97-foot whale, as "probably 174 tons," estimated by the chemist of a whaling company. But this was only approximate, as it was based on the number of cookers that were filled by the blubber, meat, and bone of this whale.

The runner-up to the record holder, weighed in 1926 at a whaling station on the Antarctic island of South Georgia, tipped the scales at 122 long tons. By the coincidence of weight, the date and place of weighing, this seems to be the same whale described in detail by Dr. Robert Blackwood Robertson in his engrossing book *Of Whales and Men*. If it isn't the same one, the weights and measures are likely for a whale of that size, and will serve our purpose in trying to see what they mean.

Blubber, flukes, fins, skull, backbone, ribs, jawbone, blood, and the internal organs—liver, stomach, intestines, heart, lungs, and kidneys—were measured and weighed separately. (Over all, the whale was 89 feet long and weighed 122 long tons. All measurements were in feet and long tons.)

The tongue weighed about 3 tons, the heart half a ton, and

---

* The international standard weight unit is a kilogram (2.2046 pounds).

the blood 8 tons! In themselves these figures are startling and of popular interest, but in addition the biologist can draw reasonable conclusions from them about function and adaptation.

Think of only the bones, for example. In this whale the skeleton wighed about 22 tons. This was 18 per cent of its total body weight, a somewhat higher proportion than in the smaller rorquals, and considerably higher than in dolphins.

In land mammals a major function of the skeleton is to support the weight of the body, and in man and some apes, in the erect position, also the weight of the head. Whales, as we have already seen, have no need for the powerful gravity-resisting force maintained by legs. Not only is the whale sustained by the buoyancy of seawater, but its resistance to gravity is more evenly distributed over its entire body. The function of the bones is not so much to carry the weight of its body as to anchor its powerful muscles. Just how powerful its propulsive muscles are you can tell by watching the swift, smooth-swimming, darting and rolling movements of the cetaceans, large and small, blues, other rorquals and porpoises alike. These powerful trunk muscles are attached to the backbone, which is made up of roughly three times as many vertebrae as in man. Because the whale's backbone is so long, markedly extended in the lumbar (lower back) region, it is not surprising that this one weighed 10 tons—nearly half the total weight of all the bones. The combined weight of the skull, jawbone, and ribs came to about another 10 tons. The rest of the skeletal weight is accounted for by the relatively shrunken forelimbs (flippers) and the rudiments of a bony tail.

It is especially interesting that, due to a difference in structure, cetacean bones are "light" in comparison with those of man and other land mammals. All have a hard outer shell that is dense or compact, and an inner core made up of lacy spongework of bony plates with blood and marrow filling the spaces between the plates. The whale's bones are remarkably light because the layer of compact bone is thin. If you keep in mind that the whale's weight is sustained by the water, you will see the importance of this difference between land and aquatic mammals.

Another striking difference between the two types of animals is seen in the amount of body fat. The whale's blubber contains at least half of all its fat, as oil, and is more than one-fourth of the body weight of blue whales, and about a third that of the sperm whales, and up to two-fifths the weight of right whales, dolphins, and common porpoises. It varies in thickness from a few to 20 or more inches and forms an insulating cover for protection in icy waters. The thickness of the blubber varies with the species, being relatively thicker in the smaller cetaceans. It varies with the seasons and it is also thickest in pregnant cows and thinnest while they are nursing their calves.

Oil is also found in the bones, and there is fat in the muscles. In the South Georgia whale the amount of oil extracted from the bones and meat together equalled the weight of that taken from the blubber. Because of this large amount of fat, the specific gravity is about 1—the same as that of water—in most cetaceans. This explains why most dead whales either float on the surface or neither sink nor rise if under water, while dead land mammals generally sink. Sperm whales and most right whales have unusually thick blubber, but once flensed their carcasses sink.

One of the perplexing facts about cetaceans is their ability to stay under water so long without breathing. Experienced sponge and pearl divers can stay submerged for up to $2\frac{1}{2}$ minutes. How long can you hold your breath, either in air or under water? One minute? Most household animals—cats, dogs and rabbits—can stay under water for 3 or 4 minutes. The muskrat can stay under for 12 minutes, some seals and beavers for 15 minutes, the sea cow up to 16 minutes, most of the larger rorquals from 20 to 50 minutes, and the sperm whale and bottlenose whale over an hour!

This makes the size of the whale's lungs of special interest. Do the lungs, for instance, carry enough air to furnish the oxygen needed during their deep dives? If so, it would seem that

Bottlenose whale (*Hyperoodon ampullatus*)

they must be proportionately larger than in land mammals. But it turns out from just such evidence as the whale weighings provide that relative to body weight the lungs of the deepest diving cetaceans are actually smaller: for rorquals, sperm whales, pigmy sperm whales, and bottlenose whales it is between .6 and .9 per cent of body weight, and for land mammals the figures are 1 to 2 per cent. In dolphins and porpoises the relative lung weights are closer to those of land mammals.

Upper jaw of a Humpback (baleen) whale showing gigantic tongue (Note also the barnacles or their scars)

In our South Georgia whale the lungs weigh somewhat over a ton, making the ratio between lung weight to body weight somewhat less than 1 per cent, but it has been found to be less in other whales. The relatively low weight of the lungs, of course, fails to answer the complex question of the whale's oxygen supply during sounding, but it has directed the search for the answer elsewhere, as you will see in the next chapter.

Now try to imagine the size of a tongue weighing three tons—as much as a small elephant! The tongue is especially well developed in baleen whales, its size being related to the type of food they eat. As the whale closes its jaws on a mouthful of seawater containing millions of tiny shrimp, the muscles of the massive tongue contract, squeezing the water through the baleen curtains and out over the side of the lower jaw. The weight of the baleen in this particular whale was a little over a long ton (2,500 pounds). This material is usually heaved overboard during the usual "dressing" process.

Another striking contrast is the size of the liver, which in this case weighed in at "only" a ton. This means that the liver is small, not only in relation to the tongue but also to the total body weight. In the average-size adult human, the liver weighs about 3 pounds and the tongue only a few ounces. Not much is known about the work of the liver in cetaceans, but there undoubtedly is an explanation for its relatively small size in this large whale, perhaps related to metabolism rate. In dolphins and porpoises the ratio of the liver to total body weight is higher.

The kidneys are among the organs that figure most prominently in the adaptation of animals to their special environments. Whales' kidneys are relatively large—about .7 to 1 per cent of body weight compared with about .4 per cent in man. These organs throw off chiefly those wastes that come from the breakdown of the body's own tissues in addition to eliminating the excess of certain substances normally taken into the body: sugar, water, and salts. It is not very probable that whales have any problem with excess sugar, since their food contains very little

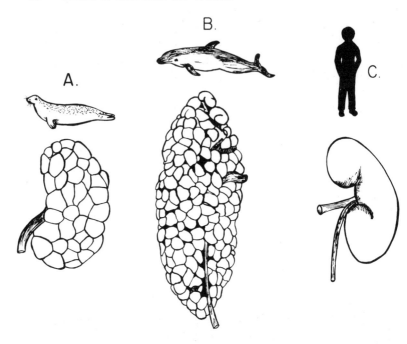

(a) Kidney of a seal; (b) of a dolphin; (c) and of a man

of it. What about water and salt? In this regard whales are like the Ancient Mariner with water, water everywhere but "not a drop to drink." In the midst of seeming plenty they can die of thirst and dehydration, just as if they were stranded in the driest of deserts. In both cases, death would come not so much from the lack of water as from the inability to get rid of salt. This is the job of the kidney, but it can do it efficiently only if it has enough fresh water to dissolve the extra salt.

So these are two more questions the biologist must ask about whales: do they drink, and if they do, what keeps them from being thirsty, since the salinity of the seawater (about 3 per cent) is considerably higher than that of their blood. In addition, their food—whether shrimp, squid, or water snails (all soft-bodied)—itself contains salt in about the same concentration as seawater. Unlike invertebrates, backboned animals, including cetaceans, have a much lower amount of salt in the blood and other body fluids than is contained in seawater. And to stay alive, the vertebrates have to maintain this lower concentration—.9 per cent, roughly 1 part in 110.

If you and I eat salty food we become thirsty and drink water or other fluids until the salt is diluted to the point of normal concentration. Then, and only then, can the kidneys throw off the extra salt dissolved in the water wastes (the urine). But what does a whale do to quench its thirst? It can drink more seawater, but this would just pile up more salt and make the whale all the more thirsty. As water is withdrawn from the blood to dilute the salt in the intestine, the whale would become dehydrated, and if this were to continue, the tissues would dry out

Kidney stone from a whale and from a man

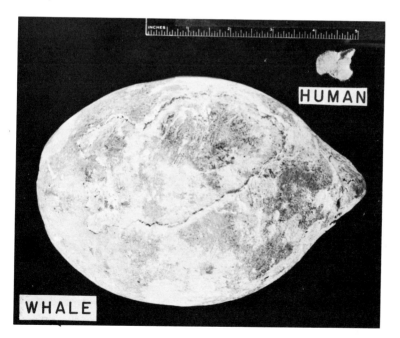

until death occurred. Since apparently this does not happen, there must be some other way in which whales handle this salt-and-water problem. For one thing, while they cannot help swallowing some seawater, they seem to get rid of most that enters their mouths with their food. Perhaps the air they breathe out contains less moisture than that of land animals. We don't really know, but we do know that whales do not have sweat glands and can't lose water perspiring.

We also know that whales have an internal source of fresh water: they produce water from the food they burn. All animals do this to some degree, one of the by-products of oxidation being water. However, more water is released from the burning of fat than from the burning of carbohydrates and proteins and, since whales burn a great deal of fat, they obtain water from normal oxidation much the same as camels, desert rats, and other animals that can go for long periods without water do. So in two entirely different environments—in the midst of the sea and in the arid desert—two kinds of mammals have this in common: a satisfactory adjustment to a scanty water supply.

While biologists believe that the cetacean kidneys must throw off a great deal of urine and thus get rid of the excess salt, there seems to be no direct evidence that this really happens. As Dr. Slijper writes: ". . . scientists' experiments tell us little on this subject, and all we really have to go by is the size and structure of the kidneys." In these respects the cetacean kidney appears to be equal to the task of excreting either a great deal of urine or a highly concentrated urine: it is exceptionally large, with a large number of lobules (tiny lobes that increase its surface), and has a well-developed cortex or outer part where secretion is most active.

Those are a few of the ways in which weighing the dead whale has helped to reveal some of the living whale's secrets.

In 1958, Dr. Slijper reported on the organ weights of 28 common porpoises and compared them with those of land mammals. The facts were in agreement with what was known about the great whales. He found that the weight of the blubber was approximately the same as in other toothed whales, but greater than in baleen whales. While the big baleen whales have comparatively small hearts, in dolphins and porpoises the heart is about the same size as in land-dwellers. The deep-diving cetaceans have relatively small lungs, but in species that live close to the surface, as do the porpoises, the lungs are about the same weight and capacity as those of land mammals. The kidneys were large, as in the other cetaceans. Certain other organs whose function is related to metabolism, which is high in whales, were also large.

4

Swimming, Diving, Blowing

HOW DOES A WHALE swim? Offhand, you might think that it swims just like a fish, using its tail (fluke) and flippers the way a fish uses its tail and fins. In the greatest of all whaling stories, *Moby Dick,* written in 1851, Herman Melville gives us an easy way to tell a whale from a large fish such as the shark: when you see the spout from the blowhole and the horizontal tail whipping the water *up and down,* it's a whale! In fact, "Thar she blows," announcing the sighting of a whale from the lookout or crow's nest of a ship, was the hunters' shout long before *Moby Dick* was written. About what fish could you say "There she blows?" None. And besides the fish's tail is vertical and lashes from *side to side* as the fish glides through the water, and this makes quite a difference.

If you watch a goldfish in a bowl you will see that its tail sweeps from side to side, and that as it swims its backbone bends sideways, in an almost snake-like fashion. So fish move easily to the right or left, but not so easily up or down. The whale's fluke, on the other hand, beats up and down; in forward motion its body is straight, and in diving or surfacing its backbone bends vertically, in somersault fashion. In fact, the English word "whale" is believed to come from "wheel" (in Norwegian it is "hwal," and in Dutch "wal") and was probably first used by sailors who had seen the whales' typical up-and-down turning motions when they were sounding for food or surfacing to breathe. The whale's ability to surface is as much a matter of life and death as its sounding to eat. Imagine what would hap-

The ten-foot-wide flukes extend from the water when the whale dives. He moves this tail up and down to propel himself through the water. The gray spots are barnacles

pen if it couldn't rise, when it had to, to "blow" and then get a breath of fresh air!

Considering its size and tightly jointed body, the whale moves with remarkable ease, grace, flexibility, and agility. Anyone who has watched dolphins swimming in a tank, or "riding the waves" off the bow of a ship, marvels at their seemingly effortless motions in rounding a curve, rolling their bodies, turning their heads for a better view (or perhaps for better hearing?), leaping out of the water, or treading water with their flukes, as Flipper does so easily. Not only the smaller cetaceans but the humpback—considered the acrobat of the big-whale clan—and the sperm whale can leap high enough to turn over in the air and swim on their backs.

Graceful motions made by dolphins: leaping
15 feet out of the water; rolling, galloping
with arched back; treading water

To understand its marvelous swimming feats, remember the
whale's streamlined features: its short neck; in those species
whose cervical (neck) bones are fused, the relative immobility
of the head; and the way the head is attached to the backbone,
the joining of the bones at the rear of the skull with the atlas
(the first cervical vertebra) permitting only a slight nodding of
the head, and even less motion sideways. Also, it cannot look
backward, but in forward propulsion this whole arrangement is
an advantage because there is nothing floppy about the head to
interfere with the streamlining. The butting often used in both
defense and attack is helped by this relative head-neck inflexi-
bility, which is further enhanced by the long spinal column with
its large number of vertebrae.

The "tail" of the whale consists of two distinct parts: the

caudal peduncle and the fluke. The peduncle—an extension of the body connecting it with the fluke—contains the same kind of caudal (tail) vertebrae as those found in land creatures with real tails, another reminder of the whale's terrestrial ancestry. These vertebrae have oblique, forward-directed projections beneath the tail, called chevrons, to which the whale's powerful lower body-propelling muscles are attached. (The upper body muscles are attached to the vertebral spines.) Compressed from both sides, the narrow peduncle completes the streamlining of the body and permits the whale to cut through the water like an arrow. The horizontally flattened, V-shaped flukes are made up mostly of soft tissues—extensions of the skin and fibrous connective tissue—with remnants of the last of the caudal vertebrae, which extend almost to the central notch of the V.

The fluke is joined to the peduncle by a "hinged" joint that makes possible not only the up-and-down swimming motion, but also the fluke's bending, tilting, and curving for all kinds of turns. All of the movements depend on the coordination of powerful muscles and tendons, also fixed to the peduncle. There are four sets of these muscles, running from the head region down along both the back and belly to the peduncle: two sets above, and two sets below. By bending the peduncle vertically and beating his flukes up and down, the whale propels himself forward. To turn, he contracts either the right or the left set of muscles, and the fluke takes the curve like a yacht before the wind. Since each of the four sets of muscles may be contracted, partially or fully, independently and in any combination, the whale can go in any direction except backward, although some of the porpoises and dolphins can back up.

Does anyone know how fast whales swim? We already know that they could not have been accurately clocked, but we do have estimates based on the observations of sailors, voyagers, and, more recently, scientists and technicians. But it's still guesswork, and moreover the speed differs with the species, and in the same species it differs under different conditions. Porpoises, chasing a school of fish or escaping the noise of an outboard motor, undoubtedly swim faster than when they are playing around a ship at what has come to be regarded as "porpoise speed"—about 12 miles an hour. Some of the faster whales could keep well ahead of the early catcher boats traveling at 15 knots* (about 17 miles an hour). Today's ships deliberately force their prey to swim faster—up to more than 20 knots— because whales can't maintain these speeds very long, and the faster they swim, the more often they have to come up for air. This is why the whalers are relentless in their pursuit, to tire them and to force them to surface more frequently for air, giving the hunters more chances at their target.

From shipboard observations, Dr. Slijper has estimated the relative top speeds for different species: 5 to 6 knots for right whales, up to 10 knots for sperm whales, 14 to 18 knots for little piked whales, 18 to 20 knots for blue whales, and 35 knots for the sei whale, the champion swimmer of the larger whales. In long distance swimming (as during migration), the California gray whale swims more slowly—at an average speed of about 2 miles an hour. Of course it plays, perhaps looks for food, and loafs along the way, so this is no indication of its top speed.

Porpoises easily keep up with ships at 20 knots, and have been recently clocked at 23 knots in an experiment in the Pacific. Aristotle was so impressed with their swimming that he regarded them as the fleetest of all animals. But we know that Aristotle had not measured the speed of a lion, which can run and leap 50 miles an hour—about the same speed as a thoroughbred race horse: nearly a mile a minute—nor that of the African cheetah, a long-legged cat that can run 70 miles an hour! But these land animals do not have to overcome the resistance of the water, so that for the size of their bodies, dolphins and sei whales are really remarkably fast travelers. They easily keep up with

---

* In nautical language, the word "knot" means "distance per hour."

modern transoceanic liners. Compared with submerged craft, they do better than the older (not atomic-powered) submarines, that have a speed of 6 knots submerged, and about 15 knots when surfaced. No wonder it has been said that whales are more efficient than submarines.

For a long time this greater efficiency (work produced by a given amount of energy) has puzzled both marine engineers and biologists. They figure that to swim 25 miles an hour the dolphin's muscles would have to generate seven to ten times the energy its muscles could actually produce! Their estimates have been based on intensive study of the work capacity of human muscle, for which reasonably definite figures are available. They assumed, of course, that all mammalian muscles—on land or in the sea—had much the same capacity as human muscles. Also, in comparisons with human athletes, it seems that dolphins have to generate more energy than their muscles are capable of producing. Or, to put it another way, compared with humans the dolphin would have to have at least seven times the muscle mass it actually has. Similarly, it has been calculated that the blue whale, swimming at 15 knots, would have to develop three times more power than seems possible from its estimated muscle mass.

Since biologists were pretty much agreed that the energy-producing capacity of cetacean muscles is not likely to differ very much from that of other mammalian muscles, they decided to look elsewhere for an explanation of the whale's efficiency. So they called in the engineers, who looked to the whale's body design for the answer.

They knew that a body cutting the water is slowed down by the particles of water immediately surrounding it. Because these water particles "cling" to it, the moving body has to drag them along with it. This is known as friction drag. If the drag of the layer of water particles nearest the body is slight, the accompanying outer layers glide over one another in what is called laminar flow. If the near drag becomes too great, the laminar flow of the outer layer particles is changed into a turbulent flow, a circular or whirlpool motion that greatly slows down forward motion.

This problem of turbulence is universal. Even the fastest jet planes have to overcome turbulence in the air. But it would seem that in the whale this problem has been solved. So the engineers' interest has a highly practical basis: what is the whale's secret; how does it manage to swim at its high speed with apparently laminar flow and no turbulence?

After many observations, both engineers and biologists decided that the whale's body design is only a partial answer to the problem, and on further investigation they discovered another lead—what looks like a built-in feature of the whale's skin. To begin with, the skin is very thin and delicate, and its surface is remarkably smooth. To some extent this smoothness would help to reduce friction at the point of contact with the water. But it didn't fully account for the speeds that the whale actually attains with its apparently limited power system.

In 1955, Frank Essapian, taking high-speed underwater photographs of dolphins in a tank at the Marineland Research Laboratory in Florida, showed that when a dolphin stepped up its "cruising" speed or, while swimming rapidly, it came to a sudden stop, wrinkles or folds appeared in its skin. This happens because the outside layer of skin is only loosely attached to the thick and tough blubber and slides over the body during high speeds. Perhaps this is how the dolphin avoids friction drag. Dr. Winthrop N. Kellogg writes in his *Porpoises and Sonar:* "Although at first glance it might appear that an uneven surface would generate more resistance than a smooth one, this is not so if the ripples coincide with the physical pressures of the water. The configuration of the skin matches the wave-form of the water, instead of opposing it."

Meanwhile, a German physicist, Dr. Max O. Kramer, had been studying laminar flow on the surface of high-speed, mechanical bodies. As early as 1938 he was granted a patent for a

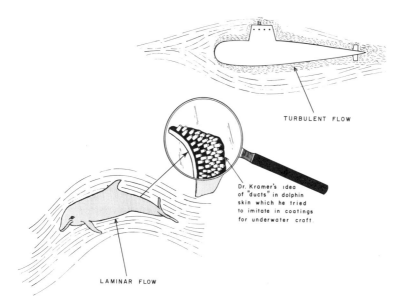

TURBULENT FLOW

Dr. Kramer's idea of "ducts" in dolphin skin which he tried to imitate in coatings for underwater craft.

LAMINAR FLOW

device to reduce friction drag, and in 1946 he was invited by the U.S. Navy to work at one of its research centers. "During the ocean crossing," Kramer later wrote, "I saw, for the first time, a school of dolphins and was fascinated by their performance." He was convinced that the dolphin's friction drag was no more than one-tenth that of the fastest man-made ships, and decided that he would study its skin, where he thought the solution to the problem might be found.

In 1955, the oceanarium, the Marineland of the Pacific, was opened at Palos Verdes, California, and Dr. Kramer sought the assistance of Dr. Kenneth S. Norris, a zoologist at the University of California who had been made curator of Marineland. From Dr. Norris he obtained samples of dolphin skin and studied them under a microscope. He found that under the brown outer skin, approximately 1/16 inch thick and so thin and delicate it could be scraped off with a finger nail, there was a yellow inner skin, about four times as thick, made up of very tough fibers. And sandwiched in between the two he saw a multitude of narrow ducts which he thought were filled with a spongy material. (We must remember Dr. Kramer is not a biologist, and his observation has been questioned.) He also found that the outer skin was waterlogged; when he dried it out it weighed only a fifth of its weight when wet, and when he put it back into the water, it again became soft as it sopped up the water. It struck him that the outer skin was a living realization of the basic idea he had tried to achieve in his patent: it acted like a smooth and pressure-sensitive diaphragm which adjusted to the waviness or turbulence of the water flowing past it. The fluid in the tiny ducts flowed back and forth as pressure changes were applied to the diaphragm, and in his words, "In this way the fluid in the ducts will absorb part of the turbulence energy, . . ." Dr. Kramer's "ducts" may have been certain blood-vessel structures characteristic of cetacean skin. At any rate, to date his work has not been repeated by cetologists.

But, following Dr. Kramer's lead, tests are being undertaken with ducted rubber coatings, filled with spongy materials, and applied to the surfaces of high-speed aircraft, submarines, and the insides of oil pipelines. The intention is to imitate the microscopic structure of the dolphin's superficial skin layers. Perhaps, in addition to forming large folds, these layers take up tiny oscillations caused by the turbulence close to the whale's body. If this should prove to be so, it would represent another adaptation to water, a feature built into the cetacean skin.

As more work is done to simulate the whale's skin, the discoveries will undoubtedly be applied to high-speed vehicles of all sorts. Dr. Slijper has expressed the hope that when such improvements are made they will no longer be needed for military purposes, and "that faster and better ships will not mean a more extensive persecution of whales and dolphins. It would be tragic, indeed, if these animals were made to suffer for the knowledge they have imparted to us."

If accurate information about the swimming speeds of

whales is hard to come by, it is just as difficult to determine the depths to which they dive. After all, think of trying to follow a whale when he suddenly decides to sound. All the more interesting are some of the ways by which the sounding depths have been estimated.

Over a century ago, in the days of hand harpooning, whalers estimated how deep a harpooned whale dived by measuring the line he pulled with him. William Scoresby, a whaling captain and a student of biology, deliberately paid out a line and estimated that the whale could dive to a depth of more than 50 fathoms, or 300 feet (a fathom is 6 feet). However, there is no sure way of knowing how much of that distance is vertical, since the tendency of a wounded whale is to swim as far away from the boat as possible, in any direction.

The sperm and the bottlenose whales—both toothed whales —are champion divers. The evidence is indirect, but it is much more conclusive than dangling a whale on a harpoon line, for remnants of cuttlefish have been discovered in the stomachs of dead sperm whales on more than one occasion, and cuttlefish— squid-like sea mollusks—live at least 250 fathoms in the deep! Since cuttlefish are part of their regular diet, these whales must regularly dive that deep for their food.

Then in 1932, by a strange accident, it was found that the earlier estimates were too low. The crew of the *All America,* a cable-layer, while at work off the coast of Colombia, South America, hauled up a section of telephone cable that needed repair. With it came the carcass of a male sperm whale which had become entangled in several hundred feet of the cable. Probably the animal had been trapped and was unable to get away, since part of the cable was twisted around its tail and some was in its jaw. The cable had been recovered from a depth of 3,500 feet! In six similar accidents, according to Dr. Slijper, the cable was at least 450 fathoms down—more than half a mile.

In 1940, the Norwegian physiologist P. F. Sholander measured the depth of the whale dive in a more scientific way. He attached pressure-measuring gauges to harpoons, and from the maximum pressures recorded on the instruments he determined the depths to which fin whales dived. These ranged from 46 to 194 fathoms, very deep for normal whales in search of food, but for injured whales under stress, as these were, the figures showed that even rorquals can dive to several times their "normal" depth.

Perhaps the most astonishing of the whale's adaptations to aquatic life are its adjustments to the requirements of deep diving. Mainly these are two: the ability to hold its breath for up to an hour, and to withstand enormous pressures. People have to withstand an atmospheric pressure of 14.7 pounds per square inch—the weight of the earth's atmosphere at sea level. For every 33 feet the whale descends into the sea, the pressure increases by an atmosphere—this same 14.7 pounds per square inch. So at 50 fathoms (300 feet) a whale is under a pressure of 9 atmospheres. Imagine the sperm whale at 500 fathoms!

To understand the extent of this adaptation, let's see how man measures up to the whale in deep diving. Pearl and sponge divers go down to nearly 15 fathoms. The record for skin divers is about 350 feet, but let's not forget that for this they need SCUBA   (Self-Contained-Underwater-Breathing-Apparatus), and even scuba diving involves hazards not encountered by the whale.

At about 100 feet the diver may begin to get giddy. While nitrogen forms four-fifths of the air we breathe, very little of it is absorbed by the blood under usual atmospheric conditions. However, at 100 feet below the water surface, the pressure is increased to three times that of air, and three times the normal amount of nitrogen is dissolved in the blood. This additional nitrogen causes the dizziness when it reaches the brain. But compared to what happens when the diver suddenly rises to the surface, dizziness is a small hazard. As he makes his ascent the pressure decreases and, like the bubbles from an uncorked champagne bottle, the compressed nitrogen expands and escapes from the blood capillaries, forming bubbles in the joints, lungs, and brain. The diver then experiences severe pain in the joints (the "bends"), difficult breathing (the "chokes"), a burning sensation in the chest and fits of coughing, and the "staggers" (blurred vision and even blackout). Together these painful and sometimes permanently damaging effects are called decompression symptoms. Also called "caisson sickness" in underwater workers (particularly "sand hogs" building tunnels under rivers and harbors), it can be prevented by gradual rising; this slows down the escape of the nitrogen so that it is eliminated without the painfully rapid expansion of the gas bubbles. (The aquanauts in the Navy's Sealab II experiment, who stayed at a depth of 210 feet for 15 days, took 36 hours to surface at the end of the experiment.)

While surfacing, the scuba diver breathes out slowly, but should he hold his breath out of panic or forgetfulness, bubbles of the expanding compressed air may block the blood vessels—a condition known as embolism. In the lungs an embolus may rupture the air sacs along with a blood vessel; or get into the circulation of the blood in the brain where it may mean death. Other possible dangers for the scuba diver are ruptured eardrums, blocked sinuses, and hemorrhages in the eyes.

None of these things happen to whales, either during sounding to depths inconceivable for a human, or during very rapid ascents. Unlike either the caisson worker or the diver, both of whom have a continuous supply of fresh air and therefore also of nitrogen, the whale takes only a fixed supply of air into its lungs, and so its blood does not become saturated with nitrogen, despite the great pressure. So when the whale ascends, only a small amount of nitrogen is present in the blood. Commenting on this adaptation, Alec H. Laurie wrote in *Nature* in 1935: "It is a most interesting fact that one of the few mammals which might run the risk of caisson sickness is just the one to have a mechanism for avoiding it."

To remain at great depths for long periods, whales fill their lungs before sounding by taking several deep breaths the way a diver does. As you have already seen, their lungs are relatively small: in proportion to their body size, whales have only about half as much lung tissue as man.

Again we are faced with a paradox: diving deeper, holding its breath longer, and taking little air with it in lungs seemingly small for its body, the sperm whale still comes to the surface in fine fettle! And when it does come up for air, it breathes at the amazingly low rate of only six times a minute! Then after about ten minutes at the surface, it may descend again to remain submerged for nearly another hour.

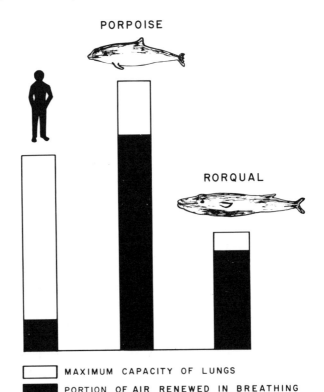

PORPOISE

RORQUAL

☐ MAXIMUM CAPACITY OF LUNGS
■ PORTION OF AIR RENEWED IN BREATHING

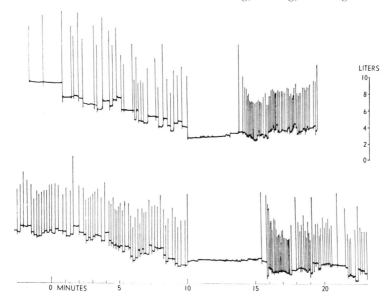

Breathing of a dolphin before and after two dives. The gap shows that there is no breathing while the animal is submerged. Note that the breathing is faster after the dive

Of course, not all whales are capable of such performances. Some rorquals and right whales are known to stay under water for 40 minutes; the fin whale (a rorqual) for 10 to 15 minutes; and dolphins and porpoises up to 5 minutes, but none of them breathe as rapidly as the average resting rate for humans (14 to 16 breaths per minute) even after fast swimming. Except for dolphins, which take from 1 to 6 breaths a minute depending on the number of dives, cetaceans are slow breathers indeed, some of the larger ones averaging but one breath a minute. To make up for their low respiratory rate and smaller lungs, the cetaceans have other ways of furnishing their tissues with sufficient oxygen for their needs.

First, their respiratory passages are designed for rapid out-flow and inflow of air. The trachea (windpipe) is short and wide; the rings of cartilage (gristle) that keep the lower airway open extend all the way to the *bronchioles* (smallest lung tubes— in terrestrial animals they are made of muscle); and the lung air sacs are very large compared with the human. These structural features allow for more complete renewal of the air in the lungs with each breath. The whale ventilates about 80 to 90 per cent!

Second, dolphins extract about twice as much oxygen from the air as we do. Taking into account only these two factors—more complete renewal of the air (about four times that of man) with double the oxygen removed—we see that one breath in the whale is equal to eight breaths in humans.

Third, in addition to being able to carry oxygen, as we do, in the hemoglobin of the blood, whales can store a goodly amount in their muscles, where it is loosely latched onto the *myoglobin,* the deep red pigment in meat.

Fourth, their muscles use less oxygen because they are under water: the suspension of breathing cuts down on oxygen utilization (breathing itself is work); the heart beats more slowly (in dolphins by about 50 per cent during diving); and, perhaps most important, underwater metabolism is changed, enabling them to release energy from the chemical splitting of stored glycogen. This chemical reaction, which occurs in the absence of oxygen, is a temporary expedient, like going into debt until the oxygen can be repaid during later breathing. This also occurs in man during extreme muscular effort, as during a 100-yard dash. In such short races, the runner holds his breath until it's over, when he breathes faster and deeper than during rest, in order to pay up the oxygen debt.

Antony Alpers, in his book *Dolphins, the Myth and the Mammal,* summarized it in this way:

. . . to put cetacean breathing in financial terms: dolphins operate on a high turnover to begin with; they extract more profits; they have better banking facilities; they can cut their overheads when pressed; and if, in spite of all this, their bank account gets into the red, they can arrange it with the accountant not to tell the manager just yet.

If there is any sight more spectacular than the dive of a whale, it is its *blow*, seen just as the colossus emerges for air. Early whalers called it the "spout" because it looked like one, the jet of vapor resembling a geyser. Heard as a loud "whoooosh," the jet rises 20 feet, straight up from the blowhole of a blue whale, obliquely from a sperm whale. So characteristic is the blow that experienced whalers can identify the species of whale by its shape and direction. Thus the right whale's blow is double and V-shaped, the rorqual's is single and vertical, the blue's is pear-shaped with the broad end at the top, and the sei's is shorter and less conical. The dolphin's blow is a puff and a sigh, and it may be accompanied by a few escaping bubbles.

The blow is the exhalation of air from the lungs, and the blowhole is the whale's "nostril." Immediately following the blow, air is drawn into the lungs in inspiration. It was once thought that cetaceans took in water during submersion and blew it out on surfacing. In fact, it has been suggested that just as a dog on a hot day cools off by taking in cool air by panting, the whale regulates its temperature with cool water. Actually, the blowholes have powerful muscular valves which are tightly closed under water, but occasionally water is trapped in the nasal cavities below the outer valve, and is then expelled during the blow. (That water does sometimes flow into the blowhole was recorded by slow motion photographs of a bottlenose dolphin.)

A better explanation is that the "spout" is a condensed vapor fountain, formed when the warm moist air forced out of the blowhole suddenly hits the surrounding cold air. The same thing happens when you *see* your breath on a cold winter's day. The whale's blow is therefore especially distinct in polar seas. But it is also seen in tropical waters, where the temperature is 100 degrees Fahrenheit. So the outside temperature cannot be the only cause of the visible spray. There must be another reason.

When the whale surfaces the gases escape from its lungs suddenly through the narrow blowhole; they cool as they expand, so even with high temperatures you can see the whale's

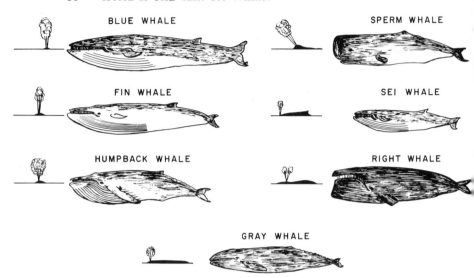

BLUE WHALE

SPERM WHALE

FIN WHALE

SEI WHALE

HUMPBACK WHALE

RIGHT WHALE

GRAY WHALE

Shapes of blows of various whales

breath. It has also been observed that when the California gray whales breathe out slowly, fewer visible droplets are formed and the blow can hardly be seen, just as it is not visible in dolphins exhaling in a tank. There is the further possibility that a small amount of water may be trapped in the nasal sacs and expelled by the force of the exhaled air, the way droplets of water are forced out when you sneeze.

The most recent study of the anatomy of the complex airway in the bottlenose dolphin shows yet another adaptation to life in the water. It has been thought that the airway was permanently separated from the food-way because when a dolphin opens its mouth for feeding under water, no water enters its lungs, and because cetaceans, unlike humans, do not breathe through the mouth. Dr. John C. Lilly, in *Man and Dolphin* says: "We have not seen an animal [dolphin] breathe through his mouth; however, we have accumulated some evidence that they can vent air through the mouth from the lungs and can even make noises through the open mouth in air."

Dr. Lilly believed he had evidence of an airway from the cetacean's mouth to its lungs that the animal cut off voluntarily. In experiments with dolphins requiring resuscitation, Dr. Lilly, among the first workers to do this, was able to insert an air tube through the mouth into the trachea. In fact, after dissecting the air passages he had decided that artificial respiration would be more difficult to carry out through the blowhole, because somewhat below the blowhole he encountered the bony separation between the nostrils. On the other hand, by pulling the larynx downward, he had a clear passage from the mouth to the larynx, trachea, and lungs. However, that the animal does this naturally has been seriously disputed. Dr. Barbara Lawrence and William E. Schevill, who have since thoroughly investigated the throat and blowhole muscles of several species of dolphins, say ". . . it seems clear that odontocetes do not voluntarily move the larynx

A pair of gray whales: one is just sinking, with much white water due to speed; the other is blowing, with blowhole open

in and out of the nares [nasal passages]." Furthermore, in an air-breathing animal adapted to living in water they question the likelihood of such an arrangement, which indeed they did not find in their dissections.

As we have seen, the blowhole opening has powerful muscles that act like valves, closing it tightly during submersion. Inside the blowhole, and on each side of the airway, there are two expandable air sacs, as well as a tongue-like projection or "plug." Below the first two air sacs and the "plug" there are two inner "lips" above two lower air sacs. These "lips" control the airway so that during expiration and inspiration they are widely separated. The upper air sacs probably collect water that may enter the open blowhole at the end of inspiration, while the "lips" below contract and discharge such trapped water. But the main function of the air sacs is probably to store air which is blown back and forth, by the contraction of the "lips," during the production of sounds.

The lower end of the blowhole is divided into two nostrils by a bony partition. These nasal cavities lead to a *glottis* that corresponds somewhat to the human voice box, except that the whale has no vocal cords. Beneath the glottis is another ring of muscle, the *nasopharyngeal sphincter,* which is open during in-

Closeup of blowhole

MARINELAND OF FLORIDA

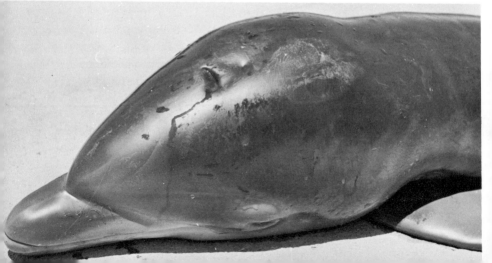

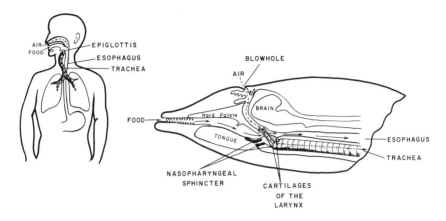

Air and food passages of man and of dolphin

spiration allowing the air to pass through the larynx into the trachea. When closed, this sphincter, along with the cartilages of the larynx, closes off the trachea from the upper nasal airway. Closure of the larynx by the nasopharyngeal sphincter occurs during swallowing, so that the food passes into the esophagus. During blowing, on the other hand, both the sphincter and valves are relaxed, leaving the airway completely open.

One of the most vexing problems in trying to study dolphins has been the difficulty in anesthetizing them safely. One of the first to undertake dolphin research under anesthesia was Dr. John C. Lilly and his coworkers, then (late 1950's) in Marineland, Florida. To their dismay the animals went into a state of asphyxia and could not be revived by artificial respiration. As Dr. Lilly later wrote in *Man and Dolphin,* "The next half hour was very painful for all of us as we watched the animal's respiration fall apart, and, finally, his heart stop." The air seemed to be leaking out of the lungs through the mouth rather than through the blowhole, and the animal was unable to inhale and restart the breathing cycle.

Dr. Lilly believed that the gradual deflation of the dolphin's lungs was caused by the leakage of air because of a loosened nasopharyngeal sphincter around the larynx. Also, since these experiments were attempted with the animal out of water, the leakage was increased by pressure on the lungs from the body weight pushing down upon them, which does not happen in the water. Even though they are air-breathing animals, this lung compression by the weight of the body, plus overheating and occasional inhalation of salt water and sand, along with sunburn and shock, undoubtedly cause the death of beached whales.

The inability of the dolphin to continue breathing normally under anesthesia remains a puzzle. In the first place, what is "normal" breathing for a cetacean? For one thing, it is not regular and rhythmical as it is in land-dwelling animals. In the latter, breathing is controlled both by nerves and by the amount of carbon dioxide in the blood supplied to the respiratory center in the brain. When you try to hold your breath in air or are forced to do it under water, you will start breathing, in spite of all your efforts to stop it, as soon as the carbon dioxide in the blood rises above a certain critical level. At present we can only guess that the dolphin is either less sensitive to a rise in carbon dioxide, or has a greater voluntary control of its breathing.

It has been suggested that the breathing center in the whale, at least in the bottlenose dolphin, is under the influence of higher centers in the cerebral cortex and therefore under voluntary control. Anesthetics that affect primarily this part of the brain may also deaden the breathing center and thus produce death by suffocation. Accordingly, Dr. Winthrop S. Kellogg in his *Porpoises and Sonar* writes: "It seems quite logical that an air-breathing mammal which lives in the sea must always be consciously aware of exactly where it is before it ever takes a breath. Otherwise, it might accidentally inspire while submerged—and so drown itself." Man, on the other hand, living in a "life-sustaining environment of air" can breathe whether conscious or unconscious, and, as we know, his breathing is safely controlled by an involuntary mechanism.

Of course it is possible that both of these factors are involved. So when given an anesthetic and made "unconscious," does the whale lose its voluntary control, and does its respiratory center become even less sensitive to accumulated carbon dioxide? No one really knows. But this is what Dr. Lilly wrote in 1961:

> As we discovered, they cannot afford deep unconsciousness at all from any cause—anesthesia, epileptic convulsions, or a blow on the head hard enough to produce unconsciousness will kill them.
>
> They do not seem to have the kind of automatic respiratory system that allows us to breathe while we are unconscious. Being under water seems to inhibit the dolphin's respiration completely, and in order to breathe and release the breathing mechanism, he must surface. An automatic breathing mechanism would bring in water and drown the animal. If knocked out, either he must regain consciousness or be carried up by fellow animals.

Early in 1965, a group of scientists—from the Communication Research Institute (headed by Dr. Lilly) and the University of Miami School of Medicine—reported on a new development. If this proves to be a solution to the anesthesia problem, it will mark a truly major breakthrough in cetacean research.

First, these scientists constructed special respiratory equipment by which they could ventilate the lungs through a tube inserted into the trachea via the mouth. The respirator was so arranged that they were able to mimic the dolphin's natural breathing pattern: they could keep the lungs inflated for any set period, and then inflate and deflate them rapidly, the way the dolphin does during normal respiration.

Secondly, they used an anesthetic which is inhaled (Dr. Lilly first had used pentobarbital, an anesthetic given by injection). This is nitrous oxide (laughing gas) mixed with oxygen in equal amounts. The animal was successfully anesthetized, felt no pain, and at the end of the experiment recovered without harm, resumed its normal breathing pattern, swam about, and took food normally. To achieve a deeper "sleep" the researchers used 70 per cent nitrous oxide and 30 per cent oxygen. At first the dolphin became somewhat agitated, trying to dislodge the artificial respirator, but it soon went under and settled down to breathing through it.

To avoid excessive pressure on the lungs because of the gravity pull of the heavy body, the experiment was performed in a specially constructed surgical tank, and the animal was kept in place with four wooden supports. Wet, heavy, rubber foam padding protected the dolphin's body from these restraining supports, and its skin was kept moist by frequent hosing with sea water.

They experimented successfully with six animals, even recording the electrical brain waves to obtain tracings called *electroencephalograms*. And under these conditions of safe anesthesia with nitrous oxide, they were able to add small amounts of the anesthetic first used by Dr. Lilly, thus inducing a deeper anesthesia, and without harm. This is indeed a feat of no mean proportions, because as the scientists say: "These methods open up the possibility of performing major surgery on this species for the first time."

5

Heartbeat Under the Sea

AMONG SO MANY who have pursued whales for scientific knowledge is an eminent heart specialist, the Boston doctor who was summoned to the bedside of President Eisenhower when he suffered his heart attack in 1955.

While still a young cardiologist, Doctor Paul Dudley White had a chance to dissect the heart of a sperm whale caught by one of the last whaling ships out of Bedford. His paper on the dissection, published in the medical journal *Heart* in 1917, gave a complete scientific description of a whale's heart. What impressed him most was the extensive conduction system, made up of specialized bands of muscle tissue, by which the heart's electrical current is spread from the auricles through the walls of the ventricles. Here he saw the "largest tissue cells ever measured" with the conductors "seemingly better perfected than in any other mammal," as he wrote in 1956 in the *National Geographic*.

Doctor White's interest in the size and beat of living things' hearts in relation to their size has never waned. He has recorded the heartbeat (by electrocardiogram) in creatures of practically all sizes, from a hummingbird to an elephant, from the tiny bird's heartbeat of 1,000 times a minute to that of Mollie, a forty-year-old circus elephant—30 beats a minutes. Most of Doctor White's studies have confirmed his belief that in both man and animals the larger the heart, the slower the pulse. But there remained to be measured "the pulse of the earth's most ponderous creature," and for Doctor White it was—and still is—a sus-

87

taining ambition to record the electrocardiogram of the great blue whale.

In 1940, plans were laid for an expedition to obtain a record of the heartbeat in one of the smaller whales—the beluga (white) whale. This species, a "dolphin in the larger sense," was selected for the first attempt because it was readily available and because it was small enough to permit Doctor White to develop a method that he hoped to use later on a large whale. (The wisdom of trying a small whale first became clear when some years later he tried to get an electrocardiogram of a California gray whale. Not only did he fail in this purpose, but some members of the party came close to losing their lives when a frightened mother whale struck their boat and put it out of commission.) The 1940 expedition was offered help by Governor Gruening of Alaska, and the U.S. Bureau of Fisheries, but World War II intervened, and the project was postponed.

Then in 1952, Doctor White, Doctor Robert L. King, a Seattle heart specialist, and James L. Jenks, Jr., president of a medical instrument manufacturing company, together arranged an expedition to Clarks Point, an Aleutian village on Bristol Bay, off the southwestern coast of Alaska. On August 6 a herd of beluga whales was located by a small airplane. In a small boat, the party drew close enough to chase the animals into shallow water, where one of the larger males was hit by an ordinary hand harpoon attached to a nylon rope. While the animal was "diving, blowing and frantically trying to escape," two special brass-headed harpoons were thrust into its back—one at about the level of the flippers, the other about three feet farther back. These barbed heads, actually electrical leads, were connected by insulated copper cables to an electrocardiograph in the boat. The thrashing whale gave the experimenters a wild ride, but despite the ride and some technical problems with broken cables, the expedition was a success. The group came away with a photographic tracing of the electrical waves of a whale heart—the first

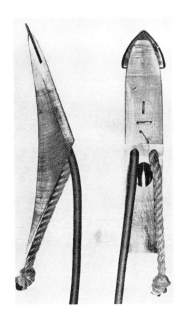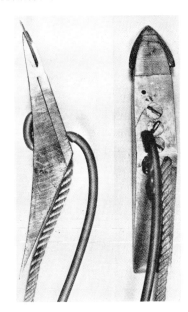

Harpoon heads used for electrocardiogram of a Beluga whale

record of the heartbeat of a large aquatic mammal in its natural habitat!

The pulse rate averaged 16 beats a minute. While this was lower than an elephant's, the whale's heart (weighing 6 pounds), was smaller than an elephant's. This was not in keeping with Doctor White's hypothesis that the larger the heart the slower its beat: for an animal the size of this whale (2,500 pounds and 14 feet long) both its pulse rate and heart weight were remarkably small. As Doctor White commented in his first report in January 1953: "The heart of the Beluga whale, the record of which we obtained, was actually not so large as that of Mollie, the elephant . . ."

While it is generally true, as Doctor White had previously shown, that the bigger the animal, the bigger its heart, and the slower its pulse (just as a large pump works more slowly than a small one) the rule does not seem to take into account the effect of submersion and diving. It has been established by other experiments that in beavers, penguins, seals, and captive bottlenose dolphins (in Marineland, Florida) the pulse rate drops sharply during diving. (In humans also the pulse rate falls during a dive.) In experiments with tame dolphins, the electrocardiograms showed a pulse rate of 110 a minute at the surface, and 50 below the surface, and the rate began to increase just before the animal surfaced. Doctor White's whale, of course, was swimming underwater—and he remarked: "It seems quite clear that an important factor in reducing the heart rate to this low figure was that of the vagal effect of diving and immersion. . ." ("vagal effect" is the slowing action of the *vagus* nerve on the heart, in people as well as whales).

In 1956, Doctor White and his colleagues, under a research grant from the National Geographic Society, embarked on an even grander adventure to obtain an electrocardiogram of a "30-ton patient." The party numbered 13, "but no one thought the number ominous," wrote Doctor White. In their 35-foot twin-diesel craft, equipped with the latest navigation devices, they entered Scammon's Lagoon in Baja California, on the Mexican coast. Here, during the early winter months, gray whales come, some to calve and others to breed. The place and weather were ideal for their purpose, which was to sink two electrodes under a whale's skin and connect the attached wires to a cardiograph. However, they forgot to take into consideration what an angry 40-foot mother could do to protect her newborn calf against all intruders, including doctors seeking to unravel the mysteries of the human heart. This tale of high adventure is told so beautifully by Doctor White and Samuel W. Matthews, on the staff of the National Geographic Society, and also a member of the unusual "whaling" crew, that we will leave it for you to read in the magazine, and cite here only their conclusions:

"We were not down-hearted. We had failed, but it was a

profitable failure, for we now knew where our shortcomings lay.

"We will surely go back . . . to record the heartbeat of the wary grays."

Let's now turn to the experience of another prominent adventurer in science who recorded the "slow thump of a finwhale's heart."

Doctor John W. Kanwisher of the Oceanographic Institute in Woods Hole, Massachusetts, had been working on survival problems of seashore animals in the Arctic but had to be content with a stranded whale for his observations of the heart. As he put it: "A live whale in the water is an imposing experimental subject. The direct approach of pursuing whales in the open sea with oceanographic vessels is too expensive . . . Such a course also might not work since whales can swim faster than most oceanographic vessels." He decided that studying a beached whale would be the next best thing. But this also was not easy; while such strandings occur fairly often on the New England coast, people in the area consider the putrefying flesh (the whales die within a day or so) a health menace and get rid of them as quickly as possible. After many disappointments, Doctor Kanwisher learned from a local newspaper of a whale beached practically on his doorstep.

In December 1959, a 45-foot male fin whale about one year old, weighing about 40 tons, was grounded on the beach at Provincetown on Cape Cod. It had been led away from shore several times, but it kept swimming back, as others have been known to do. Getting the news on a rainy Saturday night, Doctor Kanwisher enlisted the help of a physician friend, Doctor Alfred Senft, who also was greatly interested in marine research. Whatever instruments were available were hurriedly gathered: Dr. Senft brought pieces of welding rod for electrodes, long lengths of wire, and his office electrocardiograph. In the early hours of Sunday morning they (Dr. Senft was accompanied by his wife and children) reached their destination, and located the whale in the dark by the sound of its breathing! Lying on the beach at low tide, it was apparently still in good health, blowing regularly every 20 seconds.

The men, working with flashlights, located a source of power in a neighboring house to use for connecting up the electrocardiograph; they dismantled a Christmas light display for an extension cord; they took the temperature of the whale's dorsal fin and drew samples of air from the blowhole through a syringe. The incoming tide temporarily called a halt to operations, and the experimenters crawled into sleeping bags until the tide receded.

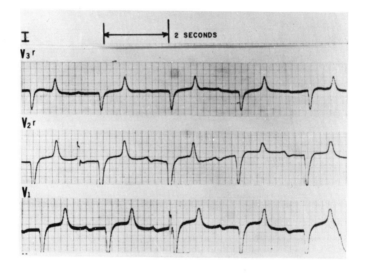

Top: Dr. Senft's electrocardiogram of the stranded Finback;
Bottom: Electrocardiogram of a man

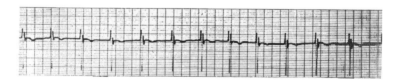

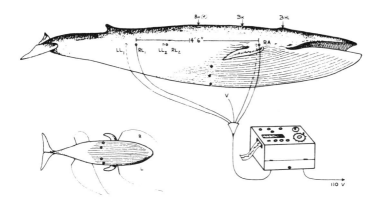

The hook-up of the electrocardiograph used by Dr. Senft

The electrodes had been pushed through the blubber into the muscle at points pretty much the same as those on which skin electrodes are placed to take electrocardiograms in humans, always remembering that the whale has no legs. The whale lived long enough for them to make recordings of its heart for several hours, expiring just about when they ran out of the ruled paper needed for electrocardiograms.

With the results of their dramatic experiments in their pockets, the two doctors drove home and examined their electrocardiogram. The pulse rate turned out to be about 27 per minute, which they thought to be nearly three times as fast as normal because of the abnormal conditions of stranding or beaching. The whale was indeed sick: there were missed heart beats in the record, and the breath samples showed impaired lung function resembling pneumonia in a human.

In subsequent conversations with Doctor Paul White, the experimenters agreed that "a record from a healthy whale in the water was still needed," and Doctor Kanwisher wrote that he regretted being unable to pursue live whales himself, "but, just in case, I am keeping an electrocardiograph ready with my temperature measuring instruments."

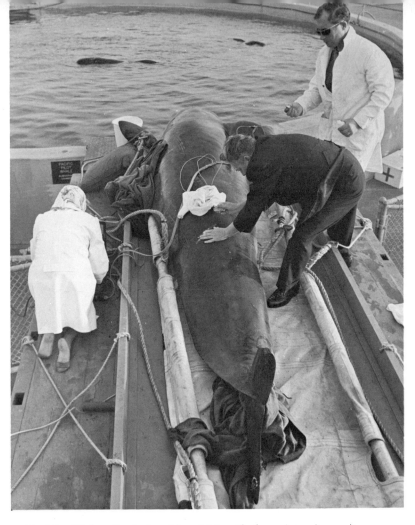

Dr. Max Weber (in dark suit) and his wife (a registered nurse)
attach leads to a Pilot whale in preparation for an electrocardiogram

Doctor Kanwisher did find out (or inferred from its
stranded condition) that the whale has a much lower heart rate
than land mammals. But how does its heart differ? Doctor
White, in measuring the heart of his early beluga whale—the cir-
cumference, thickness of the chambers, diameter of the aorta and
pulmonary artery—found that (as in other cetaceans) it was

flattened from top to bottom, broader and shorter than in land mammals. The *apex* (bottom end) was composed of both right and left ventricles, as it is in other marine mammals, while in sheep, cattle, and humans it is formed only by the left ventricle.

Further dissection showed that the valves, coronary arteries (the blood vessels supplying the heart muscle itself), veins, and the location, size, and thickness of the branches and other structures were similar to those in all mammalian hearts, including the human.

Professor Slijper has gone deeply into this subject, comparing the weight of the heart in proportion to body weight, the amount of elastic tissue in the large arteries, as well as estimating the quantity of blood and the pumping power of the heart. He has found that apart from the difference in shape (length and breadth), the whale's heart is very much like that of other mammals, and has concluded that "no single characteristic of the cetacean heart makes it more efficient or powerful than that of a terrestrial mammal—if anything, the reverse seems to be the case in the larger species."

The heart of a whale and of a man

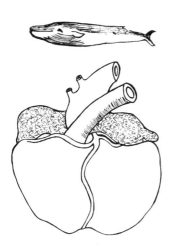

This still leaves us—despite the many adaptations we have already seen—without an explanation of underwater endurance. How does the slow-beating whale's heart supply its tissues with enough blood and oxygen during its long periods of underwater swimming?

Do cetaceans have a way of shifting their blood supply to those organs immediately essential to life—the brain and the heart—and away from, say, the skeletal muscles as has been shown in seals? There is a circulation adaptation to aquatic life which Doctor Slijper regards as "one of the strangest cetacean characteristics," a series of special blood vessel networks. The ancient observers of animals thought they were so unusual that they named them *retia mirabilia* (singular, *rete mirabile*), the Latin words for "wonder networks." Their function is still not known, but their widespread distribution in the bodies of cetaceans (they are also found in some land mammals) has led to a variety of theories about them. But, before we look into that, let's see just what the retia mirabilia are.

The retia mirabilia are masses of blood vessels arranged in thick clumps which can be seen on both sides of the vertebral column along its full length, thinning out toward the tail region and ending just in front of the fluke. Similar matted masses of these blood vessels are found along the course of the ribs. The retia are of two kinds: arteries in some clumps, and veins in others. There are no capillaries in these networks. And the retia, while linked into the circulation, are present in addition to the normal arteries, capillaries, and veins. The arteries in these networks, interposed between two regular arteries, emerge as branches of these, but can be recognized from a change in their structure: unlike the ordinary arteries whose walls contain a great deal of elastic tissue, the rete arteries have a thick layer of muscle fibers. The veins in the retia also differ from other veins, being very thin, containing little muscle tissue, and lacking valves. The absence of valves means that the blood can flow in two directions.

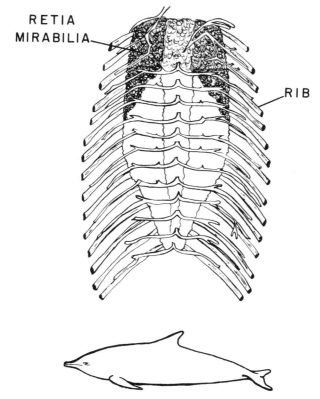

Thorax of a Common dolphin showing retia mirabilia

What could be the function of these special blood vessels? All together they constitute a perfect arrangement for alternately storing and expelling large amounts of blood. And if this is really their function, could this system account for the shifting of blood from areas where less is needed during inactivity to other parts—the brain or the heart—that require a constant supply? As yet there is no direct experimental proof that this is actually the case.

The presence of retia at the head end, outside the brain case, suggests another possible function—to prevent brain shocks from sudden spurts of blood from the large arteries. If the retia absorb the blood under high pressure in the large arteries, they could well act as shock absorbers, at the same time that the contraction of their muscular walls squeezes out the blood more evenly, as through a sponge.

Also, as we said, the retia veins have no valves. (In ordinary veins these prevent backflow of blood to the tissues and away from the heart.) The rete vessels, then, are another adaptation, since because they are of uniform diameter, there is an easy flow of blood in both directions, depending on the needs of the submerged animal.

From the location of the retia in different cetaceans, it would seem that they probably perform a variety of functions. For example, in the large rorquals and sperm whales—the deepest divers—the retia that consist entirely of veins are concentrated in the pelvic region and sex organs, while in porpoises that do not dive deeply they are found mostly in the sides of the abdomen. It has been suggested that in the deep divers those retia situated in the hind end of the body are an adaptation less to swimming at great depths than to sudden vertical movements. Doctor Slijper suggests that perhaps retia check the damaging effects of sudden pressure differences in the lungs during diving and during breathing.

There is also the possibility that the retia mirabilia help to regulate body temperature in whales. (We'll take this up later.) Perhaps these blood vessel networks are not "wonderful" in the usual meaning of the word; still they have made whale experts wonder about their exact and perhaps multiple role in cetacean biology.

Ultimately, the delivery of oxygen to the tissues depends upon its release from the red blood corpuscles whose job it is to transport oxygen. The red blood corpuscles contain *hemoglobin,* a pigment-containing protein, and it is this that gives blood its

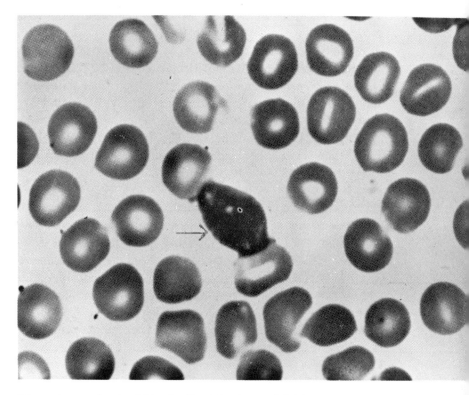

Photomicrograph of red blood cells of Bottlenose dolphin.
The arrow shows white blood corpuscle

red color. It is also the hemoglobin that readily combines with oxygen, and just as readily releases it to the tissues where the oxygen pressure is low. The whale's red corpuscles are somewhat larger in diameter than those in terrestrial mammals. This fact, by itself, would mean that a drop of blood would have fewer corpuscles and take up less oxygen than a drop of human blood of the same size, with smaller corpuscles. This is so because the larger the corpuscles the smaller the relative surface area through which the oxygen molecules have to diffuse to and from the hemoglobin; therefore, it takes longer for the hemoglobin to be saturated. However, in cetaceans there is a factor that compensates for this: the distribution of the blood between the corpuscles and the plasma (fluid part of the blood). The ratio of corpuscles to plasma in whales is much higher than the ratio in man, a way of saying that its blood is thicker. It is, therefore, possible that cetacean blood is actually richer in oxygen, though, like many other things about whales, this is by no means certain.

What *has* been definitely established is that cetacean muscles store more oxygen than those of land mammals. They contain from two to eight times the amount of *myoglobin*, a pigment which, like hemoglobin, unites with oxygen, and gives the red color to meat. Whale muscles are much darker than those of cattle or men, and so have a higher capacity for carrying oxygen. Thus, their muscles serve as chemical "reservoirs" for oxygen during submergence and particularly during diving, while the blood serves as a quick transporter of oxygen when the animal is surfacing.

6

Living Off the "Fat of the Sea"

A FEW YEARS AGO a zoology professor in California suggested a scientific investigation into the possibilities of using "whale-food" for humans. While to a scientist it appears feasible, such a project is today considered economically impractical—but who knows whether or not man may sometime need to adapt the whale's diet to his own use? If this food can sustain the largest animals ever to inhabit the earth, isn't that living testimony to the abundance of food in the pastures of the sea?

From just a few statistics on the blue whale's food consumption it is easy to see that it could hardly have survived on land and reached its present size. For example, during the first five years of its life (its growth period) it gains weight at a rate of 90 pounds a day, or 16.5 tons a year. How much does it have to eat, not only to grow at this rate, but to generate the energy it needs to breathe, digest its food, propel its huge body through icy waters, and keep constantly warm? Since the experts tell us that it feeds very little during half the year, when its food is scarce, it must eat enough during the other half to store up a reserve. And how much is "enough"? In round figures this has been estimated at about three tons a day. Even when fully grown it needs an average of a ton of food a day to maintain its bulk and to provide its muscles with the power to swim, migrate, and, when necessary, to outstrip a pursuing whaling ship. Imagine a whale having to compete with land animals that can exist on much less living space and food than the open seas provide. Against this, remember that the combined oceans cover seven-

101

tenths of the globe, and that acre for acre the sea produces five to ten times as much plant food as the land.

Of all the mammals that left the land for the sea—seals, walruses, sea otters, manatees—without doubt whales have been the most successful re-entrants. Not only are they most suitably molded to their watery environment, but here they find a rich harvest of high-protein food.

Different species of whales have different feeding habits, and peculiarly enough the giants of the clan—the blue and fin whales—live on the smallest of the ocean's inhabitants. These giants are close to the beginning of the food chain—a chain that links the most primitive plant eaters to the most complex animals, with the most finicky and exclusively meat diets.

While all whales are carnivorous (meat-eating), they can be divided into four kinds, according to the *major* kind of meat they eat: 1) plankton (the baleen whales); 2) cuttlefish (sperm and bottlenose whales and the smaller pilot whales); 3) fish (dolphins and porpoises); and 4) porpoises, seals, and other sea animals (killer whales). This doesn't mean, however, that some baleen whales, such as the sei and little piked, don't eat fish, or that some porpoises don't eat squid.

The plankton-eaters are but one stage removed from plants in the food chain: planktonic plant, to planktonic animal (shrimp-like crustacean), to blue whale; the food chain for the killer whale would be: planktonic plant, to planktonic animal, to herring, to seal or porpoise, to killer whale.

So all creatures of the sea, like those on land, ultimately depend on plants for food, either directly or indirectly, because green plants are the only *makers* of animal food.

With the aid of chlorophyll, a green pigment, sea plants manufacture carbohydrates, fats, and proteins from the raw materials: seawater, carbon dioxide, and dissolved nitrogen-containing chemicals. The energy for this manufacturing process—photosynthesis—comes from the sun's rays. To acquire this en-

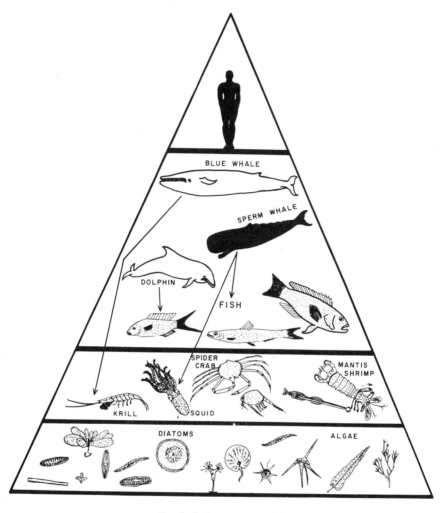

Food chain, or pyramid

ergy, these plants must live on the surface or in the uppermost, sunlit layer of the ocean.

Plant plankton consists of microscopic floating organisms,

the most important being the *diatoms*, one-celled *algae* housed in tiny, exquisitely beautiful silica shells of varied shapes: round, ovoid, star-shaped, club-shaped. The salt-water algae have been called the "grasses" of the sea, and in the pastures where they grow, animals—from the smallest to the largest—"graze." Among the floating neighbors of the diatoms are the *dinoflagellates*—chlorophyll-containing, photosynthetic *protozoa*—which also are one-celled organisms, but have, in addition, *flagellae*— tiny thread-like "organs" of motion—which they use to keep from sinking below the reach of sunlight. One-celled, but with flagellae, they form the link between true animals and the algae, true plants.

Also drifting on the surface of the sea are the dense swarms of other tiny animals: glassworms, copepods, snails, small shrimp. Together with the diatoms, dinoflagellates, and true protozoa they make up the ocean's plankton. Here, in the plankton-rich surface waters, many of the largest sea animals feed: large cartilaginous fish (basking sharks, whale sharks, and manta rays); bony fish (mackerel, herring); sea birds (penguins); and the largest of all plankton-eaters, the blue and fin whales. There are certain times of the year when these plants multiply with incredible speed, and that is why all the sea creatures have enough to eat.

In *The Sea Around Us*, Rachel Carson wrote: "The spring sea belongs at first to the diatoms and to all the other microscopic plant life of the plankton." Appearing as a living blanket of green, red, or brown, they cover miles and miles of the sea's surface. But soon comes the spawning season, and the hungry copepod, shrimp, and winged snail invade and eat their fill, but soon become the prey of larger creatures: mussels, newly spawned fishes, crabs, and tubeworms. Under this steady grazing the diatoms become more and more scarce, and for a while other forms multiply rapidly and take over whole areas of the sea. "So, for a time each spring," Miss Carson continued, "the waters may become blotched with brown, jellylike masses, and the fishermen's nets come up dripping a brown slime and containing no fish, for the herring have turned away from these waters as though in loathing of the viscid, foul-smelling algae." But in a few weeks the seas have cleared once more, after the spring flowering of the brown algae has passed.

By and large, the feeding habits of whales are determined by their mouth structure, which is also the chief basis for their classification into *Mysticetes* and *Odontocetes*. You will remember that the latter are the toothed whales, and the former have baleen and no teeth.

The baleen whales, because of their size and the strainer equipment in their mouths (see pictures, pages 107, 108, and 109), are admirably suited to feeding almost exclusively on plankton. Because of its abundance, and its rapid growth and multiplication, plankton is practically the perfect food for these enormous animals. Also, just by opening their immense jaws, the great whales can scoop up hundreds of gallons of seawater containing untold thousands of the small crustaceans. Teeth would be of little use for such a diet. In fact, the baleen whale doesn't chew its food at all: it filters it out of the water through the baleen and simply swallows it.

The particular kind of plankton that is the main food of the rorquals is called krill. In the Antarctic, where it is most abundant, it consists of a small crustacean (*Euphausia superba*) ranging in size from one to three inches in length. It is a colorful, ten-footed creature with an orange head and appendages, and a green underside. The green color showing through the thin stomach is due to the stomach's being filled with diatoms, the crustacean's food.

During the Antarctic summer, krill multiply with fantastic rapidity, so that over vast areas the sea looks like a reddish-brown soup, and ships are slowed down as they steam through the thick upper layers. It is less plentiful in the Arctic, and quite scarce in tropical and sub-tropical seas, growing best in cold waters. Krill

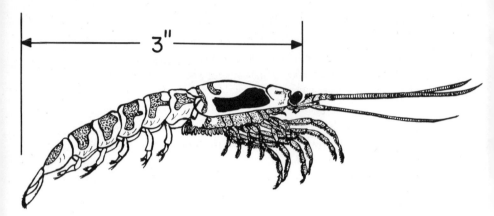

 Green [Orange pattern] **Orange**   Krill (*Euphausia superba*)

is most concentrated in the first five fathoms, where the whales gather it in, but it has been found as far down as 500 fathoms, where it may be food for other sea creatures.

When a whale's stomach is opened for inspection on board ship, a hundredweight or more of the little shrimp may spill out on deck. The smaller ones are one year old or less; those about three inches long are at least two years old, since it takes two years for them to reach maturity after hatching. It is from krill, and in turn, through the food chain, from diatoms, that the whale derives its blubber oil that eventually, in factories, is made into margarine and soap.

The orange color of krill is due to *carotene,* the forerunner of vitamin A, abundant in the whale liver and to some extent in the blubber. A number of conservationists have proposed that we go directly to the source of the oil and spare the whales, since it is chiefly for the oil that they are hunted. But as yet this attractive idea has not been pursued because of the cost of extraction of oil from the krill, a job that the whale does so efficiently. Dr. Slijper points out that atomic power may some day solve this problem, but there remains the problem of tracking down krill concentrations. Apparently the whale has some means of locating the densest krill swarms without difficulty—perhaps by the sounds the crustaceans are said to make.

Let's see how these gigantic whales handle a mouthful of their tiny prey. The baleen has been likened to vast string-curtains hanging from the upper jaw—the baleen plates. The baleen plates, made of a material like that of nails and horns, are less than one-fifth of an inch thick, and each plate is less than a half inch from the next. They have hairy fringes at the lower end and the fringes are interwoven to form a coarse fiber mat that acts as a strainer. Functionally, the whole straining apparatus is like a net with very fine holes through which the seawater flows out

Fin whale, showing eye and upper part of head at right, ventral grooves at top left, line of lower jaw and baleen plates at bottom center

Humpback whale, showing outer view of baleen. The hairs show only at the tip. The whale is on its back, the lower jaw uppermost

freely while the krill is held back. As the whale closes its mouth, the large soft flabby tongue presses down on the contents of the mouth, forcing streams of water out between the plates, while the fiber mat holds in the shrimp.

The baleen of right whales is long and narrow, reaching an average length of 10 feet in the Greenland whale. In these whales the baleen has also become arched and follows the contour of the head. In rorquals the baleen is much shorter and wider, from about three feet long in the blue whale to somewhat over a foot in the California gray whale. The number of plates also varies from about 300 in the humpback to over 400 in the blue whale. The plates are constantly worn down by friction with the water, the tongue, and the shrimp, just as our nails wear

Top: Fin whale, showing hairy inner surface of baleen. The lower jaw has been removed; picture shows the roof of the mouth;
Bottom: Fetus of a Bryde whale. The baleen has not yet grown, but the ventral grooves, lower jaw, and tongue show clearly

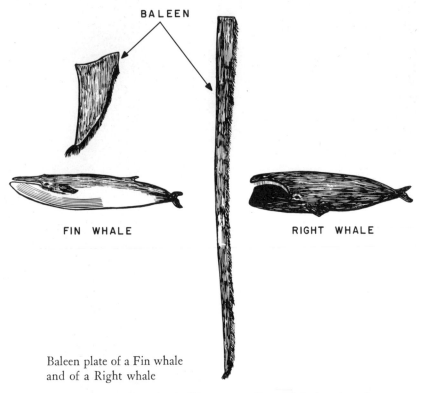

BALEEN

FIN WHALE

RIGHT WHALE

Baleen plate of a Fin whale
and of a Right whale

down at the tips. And, like our nails and hair, the plates are
constantly pushed out by growth at the roots, from cells in the
whale's gums. Unlike hair, baleen does not become gray but
thickens with age. Also the thickness of the horny material varies
with certain conditions: nutrition, sexual events such as ovulation, birth, weaning, etc. This results in the formation of ridges
and grooves, similar to the annular rings in the horns of cattle,
which can be used to get a rough estimate of the age of the
whale.

　　While no one has ever seen exactly what happens inside the
mouth of a large whale when it swallows, some differences are
known to exist between the right whales and the rorquals. In
the former, after the mouth is closed, the tongue is brought up

and the krill pushed toward the throat. In the rorquals, it is believed the large external folds and grooves on the underside of the lower jaw unfold, greatly enlarging the mouth cavity. As the mouth is closed, the muscles of the tongue and the base of the mouth contract, expelling the water over the edge of the lower jaw. In the right whales, however, the water has been seen to stream out, even as the animals are swimming with almost constantly open mouths, scooping up krill as they swim. At intervals, apparently when they have enough food for a mouthful, they close their mouths and swallow.

Practically the only food found in the stomachs of whales caught in the Antarctic is *euphausia* krill, although occasionally other animals—an occasional fish or penguin, perhaps accidentally sucked in— are swallowed.

The humpbacks and little piked whales vary their krill diet with herring, mackerel, whiting, and cuttlefish (a deep sea mollusk). One humpback was found with a cormorant stuck in its throat; in Bryde's whales,

An Antarctic species of Little Piked whale (*Balaenoptera acutorostrata*) that does not have white on its flipper

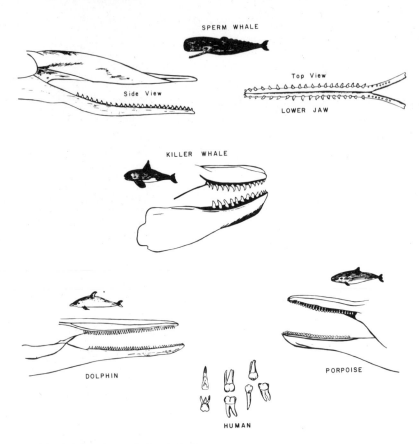

Teeth of various whales and of man

small sharks and, in one instance, fifteen penguins were discovered. Since penguins themselves hunt for fish, it is easy to see how this could have happened.

The ancestors of modern whales had several kinds of teeth —canines, premolars, and molars—suggesting that their diet was not limited to fish. Modern toothed whales are mostly fish eaters, and for this diet two long rows of even, conical teeth—slightly hooked pegs that secure the captured fish in the jaw—are ideal equipment. Only in porpoises is the tooth spade-shaped, and often tricuspid (three-pointed). Cetaceans grow only one set of teeth; unlike humans they don't shed their "baby teeth." (You may know that sharks shed their teeth constantly, covering the floor of the ocean with the discarded ones, as they are replaced with new ones.) In older animals the crowns are worn down, the protective enamel is almost gone, and the bone is exposed.

When the mouth is closed, the teeth in both jaws interlock. As mentioned earlier, it is interesting that only within recent times has it been discovered that sperm whales also have teeth in the upper jaw, but often they are deeply imbedded and hidden in the gums.

The single roots of Odontocete whales' teeth are so firmly attached to the tough gum tissue that they are dislodged only with great difficulty. When sperm whaling was in its heyday, whalers would while away the time by carving designs of a ship or the form of a favorite lady on the three-inch tooth—a craft known as "scrimshaw." But first they had to wrest the firmly imbedded tooth from its moorings in the jaw.

For its size (50 feet in average length), the sperm whale has

Dolphin shows its teeth while "laughing" at its director

Octopus

small teeth. Yet they are adequate for holding the soft-bodied creatures on which it feeds. The sperm whale's favorite food is cuttlefish—a name sometimes used to mean squid, octopus, and other tentacled mollusks—but it doesn't scorn other prey, such as an occasional seal or ten-foot shark, as well as skates and other fish.

The sperm whale's favorite kind of squid is the giant, with tentacles 10 to 12 feet long. These mollusks are themselves flesh eaters, living on crabs, lobsters, and other arthropods (creatures with jointed legs), which they kill by releasing a poisonous secretion from their salivary glands. Some species of octopus can inflict painful bites with their beaks, killing and tearing their prey apart, but other species are shy and inoffensive.

Equipped with an ink sac, the octopus releases a thick,

black liquid when alarmed. This not only distracts its pursuers but paralyzes their organs of smell, throwing them off the scent. To move—and it can move very rapidly—it uses a thick muscular structure called the mantle that is fitted with a funnel-shaped opening, the siphon. It fills the mantle cavity with water and forcibly ejects it from the siphon, in this way achieving jet propulsion in a direction opposite from that in which the funnel is pointed.

The chief offensive (and defensive) weapons of these mollusks are their long tentacles—eight in the octopus and ten in the giant squid. The tentacles are covered with sucker disks with which the animal fastens itself onto its prey. The octopus may cause harm to animals much larger than itself, including sharks and sometimes even the sperm whale.

The sperm whale, you will remember, is the champion diver, at least as far as depth of sounding is concerned, and down in the deep he invades the home of the tentacled cuttlefish. Both the octopus and giant squid have been found in the stomach of sperm whales. There is no contest with the smaller prey—about three feet long—but encounters with a giant squid may mean a real battle.

The weaponry of both adversaries is formidable, and the outcome is not always immediately in the whale's favor. If it comes upon its prey from behind, unseen, the whale has the advantage. It seizes its captive in its huge jaws and swallows it whole. There is at least one authenticated case of a giant squid found in the stomach of a sperm whale, intact with tentacles. The squid was 35 feet long and weighed 400 pounds!

In the struggle for life in the open sea the most powerful and the fleetest tend to win out, even against the most complex defenses, as in the case of the sperm whale and the giant squid. Because the squid is equipped with good vision, and a well-developed nervous system—giant nerves that carry impulses rapidly —it reacts with fast reflexes in catching its food. This has given these animals a reputation for "intelligence" as well as ferociousness. Marine biologists have often pointed out that both qualities are exaggerated, just as is the "voraciousness" of the sperm whale, which actually is considered inoffensive except when molested or threatened. Then it has been known to ram boats and even larger vessels with its immense head or powerful tail. Moby Dick had his counterpart in history: in 1820 a sperm whale stove in and sank the *Essex,* a Nantucket whaling ship.

There is, however, one species of whale that habitually preys upon other warm-blooded animals—the killer whale. Really a large dolphin, the killer was classified by Linnaeus as *Orcinus orca,* and by Cope as *Grampus rectipinna.* This is why you sometimes see it referred to as Orca and sometimes as Grampus. But to avoid confusion with the much smaller Risso's dolphin (*Grampus griseus, not* a close relative), it is simpler to call it by its common name—killer whale.

The killer is easily identified by conspicuous white markings against the background of its coal-black skin, and its high, triangular-shaped dorsal fin. Found in all the oceans, the male grows up to 30 feet in length, the female to less than 20. In addition to porpoises, and whales larger than itself, the killer feeds on seals, walruses, sea-birds, fish, and squid.

An example of their tactics was seen in the fall of 1947 by one of the divers from Marineland of the Pacific, while he was working aboard a tuna clipper off Baja California, Mexico. He saw 15 to 20 killers attack a school of about 100 dolphins, and later reported:

. . . the killers swam in circles around the dolphin school, gradually crowding them tighter and tighter. Finally one of the killers veered off, rushing at the school, while the others continued circling. In this fashion, the killers ripped at the school one at a time, killing many of the dolphins. The water was red with blood.

The most famous record of the killer's appetite is the oft-repeated story of a 24-foot whale in whose stomach the remains of 13 porpoises and 14 seals were found. And Dr. Slijper tells of one caught off one of the Pribilof Islands in the Bering Sea whose stomach contained remains of 32 baby seals. The killers also prey on belugas, narwhals, and dolphins.

The killer will attack even the largest of the blue whales. A young blue may be taken on by a single killer, but for an adult giant the killers band together to tear at the flippers and the lips (seemingly to get at the tongue), and after destroying the mouth they leave the victim to die of loss of blood. Then they consume the rest of the carcass. The California gray whale is said to be so frightened of killers that it is paralyzed into inaction; it simply turns over, belly up, helpless before the attackers.

Many stories are told of killers following factory ships to feed on the tied-up whale carcasses before they are pulled up on the skidway for flensing. A whaler rarely misses the chance to fire at a killer in sight of the ship, but even gun-fire doesn't frighten them off. Fishermen have their own reasons for hating them because they break the nets to get the fish, causing severe economic losses. Like other whales, they swallow their prey whole or in large pieces, but as Dr. Slijper points out, "the claim that the Killer slits its victims' bellies open must be dismissed as fable."

A recent account in *Rod and Gun* tells also of what appeared to the observer as one of their aggressive methods of seeking food. A photographer for the British Terra Nova Expedition

California Gray whale (*Eschrichtius gibbosus*)

was standing on the Antarctic ice when eight killer whales came up under the ice, breaking it with their heads and backs and leaving him stranded on a small floe rocking under his feet. The whales shoved their heads out of the water and, as the photographer leaped from one floe to another, they followed him hungrily, he thought. Luckily a current separated him from his pursuers just in time. Glancing back, the photographer saw one of them "looking around with its little pig-eyes to see what had become of me." But marine biologists would probably say that the killer mistook him for a penguin, just as we say that a penguin looks like a man in evening dress.

Actually, the killer whale is not a "man-eater;" there are no "man-eating" cetaceans. This brings up an old question: was Jonah really swallowed by a whale? If he was, what kind of a whale could it have been? In the *Book of Jonah* it is related that "Now the Lord had prepared a great fish to swallow up Jonah. And Jonah was in the belly of the fish three days and three nights." We have to assume that the term "fish" was used in its general meaning of a sea-living creature. Of course, the white shark is indeed a man-eater, mangling its victim; but that would not fit into the story of a three-day sojourn in its body.

To try to clarify the Bible story of Jonah, Roy Chapman Andrews decided on an incredibly direct way: "So I pushed my body partly down the throat of a dead 60-foot sperm whale [which has an enormous throat]. I could just squeeze through. A fat man couldn't have made it. But of course a man would be dead long before he got into the stomach."

This fate, for any man who somehow got into a sperm whale's mouth, has been attested to by an eye witness. In the June 1947 issue of *Natural History Magazine,* Dr. Egerton Y. Davis of Boston described an incident that occurred when he was aboard a sealing vessel out of St. John's, Newfoundland, over half a century before he sent the letter to the magazine. "The whale was apparently as lost and out of season in those Arctic waters as he was confused and angered by the sudden appearance of a fleet of ships and men," the doctor reported. In full view of the crew of one of the vessels, a sailor became separated from the rest on an ice floe, fell into the water close to a sperm whale, and somehow was swallowed. The whale was immediately killed by a shot from the ship's cannon, and after many hours of hard work the men hacked their way through its abdomen. The doctor removed the man's body, but "the appearance and odor were so bad that all save I were forced to turn away, and we were obliged to consign him to the briny deep" because preservation for a later burial in his home town was impossible.

So while it is indeed possible for a sperm whale to swallow a man, he could hardly be expected to emerge alive. Assuming that he was swallowed alive, missed the whale's teeth on his way in, survived asphyxiation in the whale's stomach, and then the whale spewed him out, "science can grant him only three minutes, not three days. If Jonah's voyage lasted as long as that, it was indeed a miracle," wrote Arthur C. Clarke, in an article in *Holiday,* March 1962, in which he discussed Jonah and the whale.

Among the smaller toothed whales are the beluga and narwhal, both deep water feeders. They live on a mixed diet of cuttlefish, shrimp, crab, and fish. The beluga has eight to ten teeth on each side of its lower jaw, but narwhals have no teeth at all, even though the embryos start out with four tooth buds, two on each side of the upper jaw. However, the fully developed male of

Narwhal (*Monodon monoceros*)

Ganges River dolphin (*Platanista gangetica*)

the species grows one eight-foot tusk that grows out from one of the buried teeth on the left side. The strange thing is that the narwhal does not use its tusk as a weapon even in mating battles. If the tusk breaks off it is likely to become infected, since all the way to the tip it contains dental pulp, which unlike that of the elephant's and the boar's tusk, is living tissue. Perhaps instinct warns the narwhal not to use its tusk. Since only the male has a tusk, it may serve simply to distinguish its sex, as antlers mark a male deer, or a beard distinguishes a man.

An interesting adaptation to a different environment is seen in the fresh-water Gangetic dolphin of the Ganges River and its tributaries, where it feeds on fish and crabs. It has a beak shaped like a forceps and teeth in both jaws, which it uses to stir up the mud in search of food. To help in this, its neck is longer and more flexible than in ocean-dwelling dolphins.

When wild in the sea, porpoises and dolphins are perhaps the most finicky of eaters, living exclusively on live fish. Mullet is a favorite (the fish mostly fed them in captivity), but they also like herring, mackerel, blue runners, and butterfish. Traveling in packs, porpoises will round up a school of fish very much the way cowboys round up a herd of cattle. Naturally commercial fishermen don't like them and have given them the reputation of being heavy eaters, but this is disputed by naturalists who have studied dolphins at close range. Capt. William B. Gray comes to their defense:

Some fishermen libel the porpoise by claiming they eat their weight in game fish every day. This, of course, is erroneous. We

Right: Diver hand-feeding dolphins under water; Above: Dolphins leaping into the air to be fed

stuff them with all the fish they will consume five times a day at the Seaquarium, and the average full-grown bottlenose will eat no more than twenty-five pounds of fish in a day. We are quite certain that there are many days they do not catch half that amount in their natural element. . . .

What fishermen have to contend with is not so much porpoises eating their catch, but rather the damage they do to the nets and, by ripping the nets, releasing the fish. One such incident is vividly described by Thomas Helm, a shark fisherman, naturalist, and writer:

A herd of porpoises came puffing and blowing into the bay . . . one porpoise, which would have weighed hardly more than fifty pounds, suddenly leaped clear of the water and landed inside the net [set out by the crew of a mullet boat]. Instantly he became excited, rushing into the cotton mesh at first one spot and then another in an effort to get free and rejoin his family. . . . All at once the adult porpoises decided to rescue the youngster, and one after another ripped into the net. At times they would drag it for a full fifty yards before backing off for another try. Now and then one would become enmeshed, and in a wild fury of rolling, thrashing and tumbling, scores of feet of expensive gill netting was ripped asunder. . . . As a fellow human, I could actively hate the destructive porpoises. As a naturalist, I in turn admired the way the porpoise family was fighting relentlessly against the net, which to them must have represented a mysterious foe that held an offspring captive.

On the other hand, we are still mystified by the behavior of Namu, described in Chapter 1. Towed in his makeshift pen, and escorted at times by 30 or 40 other killers—including a female and two calves—he could have broken out of captivity or been released by his companions. Instead, there were only "vocal" exchanges. What was the meaning of their "conversations"? Did they "decide" on a peaceful and resigned acceptance of a strange situation?

* * *

Since cetaceans swallow their food without chewing, no digestion takes place in the mouth, as it does in man. In fact, most whales either have no salivary glands at all or only rudimentary ones, so their digestion begins in the stomach. This is made up of three compartments, resembling that of ruminant animals such as the cow, rather than the single-pouched stomach in humans. The first compartment—the forestomach—contains no glands and produces no digestive juice. Like the paunch or rumen of the cow's stomach, the forestomach has a thick muscular wall, but here the resemblance ends. In cattle this part of the stomach contains millions of single-celled organisms whose enzymes partly break down their hosts' food; in some whales, on the other hand, the forestomach occasionally contains sand and small stones which, together with the powerful stomach muscles, help to crush the food. In addition, the crustacean shells of the krill eaten by plankton-feeding whales, and the vertebrae of fish eaten by toothed whales, add to the bulk of food-grinding aids. Like birds that swallow their food whole and grind it with the help of pebbles in the crop, so whales "chew" their food with their stomachs. It is interesting that those whales whose food is exclusively the soft-bodied cuttlefish—all beaked whales (*Ziphiidae*)—lack this first compartment.

Outline of the stomach of a Beaked whale, a man, and a Bottlenose dolphin

BEAKED WHALE

BOTTLENOSE DOLPHIN

BOTTLENOSE DOLPHIN

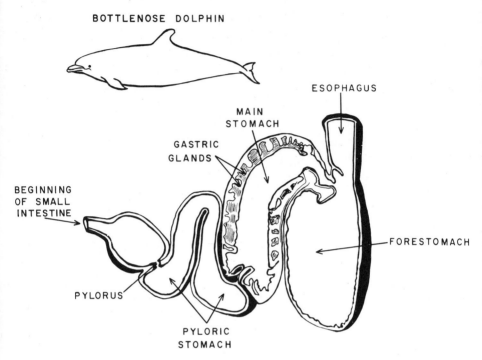

Three-compartment stomach and pylorus ("gate" to the intestine) of a Bottlenose dolphin

As the crushed food passes into the second compartment—the main stomach—it is mixed with secreted juices and digested by enzymes: pepsin, a protein-splitting enzyme, and lipase, a fat-splitting enzyme (in adult humans this is formed in the pancreas). In addition to enzymes, this compartment contains hydrochloric acid (as in human stomachs). The third compartment—the pyloric stomach—also has glands, but seems to contain little or no acid.

The whale's intestine is proportionately longer than that of man and land-dwelling carnivores. While a man's intestine is 5 to 6 times the height of his body, the intestine of sperm whale is about 24 times as long, and of dolphins about 12 times. Dolphins and baleen whales have only a very short *cecum,* the sausage-shaped first section of the large intestine. All other cetaceans have no cecum, nor appendix, so that the small and large intestines are almost identical.

Cetaceans also have no gallbladder, which in other mammals stores and concentrates the bile produced in the liver. The importance of this deficiency is not known, except that bile flows continuously from the liver into the intestine without being stored. The large amount of fat in the whale's diet may account for the uninterrupted supply of this secretion, which is essential to the digestion of fat. Because the whale has no gallbladder, it also has no trouble with gallstones. When such stones enter the human gallbladder duct, they cause great pain and have to be removed surgically. But the sperm whale does form a substance called ambergris, a wax-like, dark brown, pliable material sometimes recovered from its intestine. Ambergris was once highly prized by whalers for it brought its weight in gold as an essential ingredient of perfumes (it is still used, but synthetic products have greatly reduced its value).

In the American Museum of Natural History in New York, in a case next to the model of the blue whale, there is an odd assortment of pebble-sized lumps collected by people who thought they had found a fabulous treasure; unfortunately, none of these was ambergris.

7

Always Warm, But Never Hot

"MAN OVERBOARD!" The dreaded cry, ringing out on a whaling ship in the Antarctic Ocean, awakened the crew, but by the time they got help to him he was unconscious, though he had been in the icy waters for only 15 minutes. This is about as long as a human being can live in water at freezing temperature—32 degrees Fahrenheit. The man who went overboard never recovered. Even in water of 50 or 55 degrees, humans lose consciousness after two or three hours. But most whales, except for some dolphins and the Bryde's whale, which live in warm waters, spend at least half of their lives at polar temperatures. They are almost constantly exposed to an environment that is 50 degrees or more lower than their own body temperature. What prevents whales from being chilled to death?

It's just about as difficult to take the temperature of a whale at sea as it is to weigh it on a ship's deck. But from the temperatures taken of freshly killed whales, when the bodies were still warm, the normal temperature of a whale seems to be about 96 degrees. There is one record of a temperature of nearly 101 degrees in a living sperm whale that had been paralyzed by a harpoon after a strenuous chase.

Recently the body temperature of a bottlenose dolphin was recorded by radio transmitter while it was swimming freely in a pool. The transmitter was inserted into a dead fish through the gills, and the dolphin swallowed the fish whole. The transmitted signal was easily detected under various conditions, including removal of the dolphin from the pool on a stretcher, and by suitable electronic devices these signals were translated into degrees of temperature. The results of these experiments, done in a laboratory at the University of California in Berkeley, showed that the dolphin's temperature varied between 96 and 99.5 degrees, depending on changes in the temperature of the water, the swallowing of cool liquids, taking the animal out of the water, or training experiments.

Both these extremes of temperature—96 and 101—are within the range of warm-blooded animals. The question is: how does the whale stay warm and yet not overheat in the cold ocean? Before answering that, let's see how man regulates his body temperature.

Let's suppose that on a hot summer's day you and your dog jump into the water for a swim. Your first feeling is: "Gee it's cold!" And if you just stand around in the water you feel all the colder. But you know that you don't stay still for long. You start to swim, and as you swim you warm up. Even then someone might tell you that your lips are blue and that it's time to come out.

In order to feel warm again, you and your dog need to dry off. The dog shakes his fur to get rid of the water, and you rub yourself down with a towel. If you didn't, you wouldn't get warm so fast because the water would keep on cooling your body by conducting heat away from the skin. (Some water mammals achieve the same thing because of their waterproof fur; others by drying their fur the way your dog does. But the whale has no furry protection, and does not leave the water.)

We cool off in water and warm up while swimming. We get overheated while running and cool off by sweating—something a whale can't do because it has no sweat glands. It's a case of balancing the heat produced by motion with the heat lost— mostly through the skin. The result is an even, balanced body temperature. It's like keeping water circulating in a tank at the same level: the amount of water that goes out the outlet pipe must be made up for by the amount coming in through the inlet pipe. Actually, the way body temperature is regulated is far more complex, even more complicated than the way the air in an industrial plant, or even your own home, is thermostatically controlled at a set temperature, for the body is a highly sensitive living organism, with countless factors all working together.

The body's heat comes from the oxidation, the flameless burning, of food. Most of this takes place in the muscles, some of it in the liver and other glands, and the rest in all the other cells in the body. Even when you are asleep or just lying in bed, the heart and the muscles of respiration and digestion are continually working and giving off heat. If you are cold and you shiver, your teeth chatter, and your muscles, involuntarily spurred into action, release heat. Shivering is the body's automatic way of increasing the body's heat production.

The body also conserves heat. The "goose flesh" or "goose bumps" you sometimes get when you are cold are caused by the involuntary contraction of the tiny muscles that make the hairs on your arms appear to stand on end. It doesn't help you much in conserving heat, but for furry animals the trapped motionless air is a very useful blanket protecting against too much heat loss.

Another—and more effective—method of heat conservation is through a system of nerves that control the size of the small blood vessels in the skin. When you go out into the cold, these blood vessels partially close, less blood reaches the body's surface—the skin—and so less heat is carried away from the blood. The less blood there is in the skin, the less will be delivered also to the sweat glands in the skin. So in winter your sweat glands are less active, and because you sweat less there is less evaporation; and since evaporation—the conversion of water to vapor— takes heat from the body, less sweating means less heat loss.

The same system of nerves keeps you from overheating on a hot day by opening the blood vessels in the skin. These nerves become less active when warm air surrounds the skin, so more blood is brought to the surface of the body and the blood is cooled. Also, sweating means more loss of heat by evaporation of the sweat. You also lose heat by warming the air you breathe in, and by the evaporation of moisture in the air you breathe out. When you eat cold foods you lose heat by warming them, and you lose still more when you eliminate warm wastes.

These are some of the ways by which the sensitive balance of body heat is automatically maintained. This balance, the normal body temperature, is upset only when you are sick and have a fever, or when you are exposed to very low temperatures for a long time.

But animals have many other ways of adjusting to changes in the environment temperature. Cats, for example, have no sweat glands but they increase their heat loss on a hot day by more rapid breathing. Also, you may think your dog is uncomfortable (and perhaps he is), panting with his mouth wide open and his tongue hanging out; actually he is keeping cool! He finds a shady spot and sprawls out, because by stretching out he makes it possible for more heat to escape from a larger body surface. By rapid breathing and increased exposure of his tongue and the moist lining of his mouth, he increases evaporation and heat loss. On a cold day, on the other hand, he hunches and curls up in a corner, exposing the least amount of surface through which heat might be lost. In doing this, his muscles are also stimulated to produce more heat. If he has his own house, the kennel air itself warms up with this heat, just as the air in a barn is warmed by the cows' and horses' own body heat.

Of course, man does not depend entirely on automatic body mechanisms: he builds shelters to keep the surrounding temperature at a comfortable level, and he wears appropriate clothing. When the temperature is 70 to 75 degrees, there is the least strain on the body, both for keeping warm in winter and cool in summer. So when out of doors in winter we wear more clothing, and we choose the kind of clothing that will reduce the body's heat loss to a minimum, such as woolens, furs, and woven synthetic materials—all poor conductors and thus good insulators. Linens and cotton are good conductors, and so are worn in summer to permit body heat to escape. In summer, fans create air currents that help both heat conduction and evaporation of sweat; in winter, double windows and storm doors cut down drafts from the outside and reduce heat loss from the house. Today, in our country, air conditioning and central heating can control the indoor temperature so that it's practically constant all the year round.

In whales, heat production comes from the same kind of internal combustion engine as in humans—chiefly from the muscles and certain glands—with the fuel coming from their food. But there is a very important difference in the amount of energy the whale requires to keep warm.

Whales have no regular sleeping time, as we do, of about eight hours for every 16 hours of wakefulness, although they do sleep at intervals. The sperm whale apparently has deep sleep spells; dolphins and pilot whales are often seen gliding with eyes closed.

For most of us only part of our time awake is spent in intense activity. You may spend a few hours in hard play, but you sit perhaps twice as long, in school and studying at home. When you are active, you use up 2,500 to 3,000 Calories a day. About 1,600 to 1,800 of these are needed just to keep your body alive: to maintain normal temperature, to breathe and digest food, and to circulate the blood while you are at complete rest. And unless you do the hardest physical work, you expend only 800 to 900 additional Calories.

But the whale has an entirely different problem in maintaining its energy needs. If you can watch a dolphin in Florida's or California's Marineland, or in the New York Aquarium at Coney Island, you will see that it is in active motion almost all of the time, and probably so is a large whale in the open seas, with only odd intervals of inactivity. Marine scientists have made estimates of the blue whale's energy needs. If its muscles are as efficient as human muscles, the blue whale requires more than

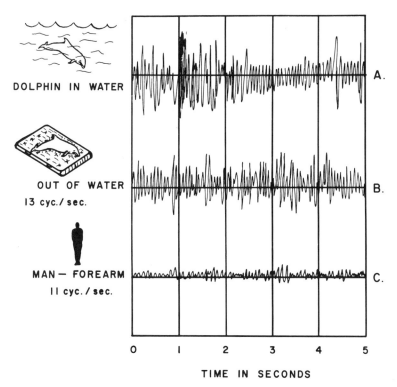

DOLPHIN IN WATER   A.

OUT OF WATER   B.
13 cyc./sec.

MAN — FOREARM   C.
11 cyc./sec.

TIME IN SECONDS

Height and number of microvibrations: (A) Dolphin in water;
(B) Dolphin on a mattress, out of water; (C) Man's muscle
vibrations on the same mattress

three times the amount of energy to swim at four knots (probably its minimum speed) as it does to maintain its basic needs of
keeping alive. Roughly, the energy needs for a 90-ton whale are
780,000 Calories a day for propulsion, and 230,000 Calories for
keeping an even body temperature, for breathing, and for digestion. At higher swimming speeds—up to 15 knots—of course, the
whale must spend much more than three times as much energy
swimming as it does in just staying alive.

Not only do whales, like people, increase their energy production by moving about faster, but there is now evidence that dolphins also shiver, involuntarily increasing their heat production. When a dolphin was kept restrained in water at 52 degrees, it noticeably shivered. In addition, two scientists at the University of California in Los Angeles recorded the microvibrations that occurred in the dorsal body surface of a bottlenose dolphin when it was swimming and when it lay on a foam rubber mattress out of the water. It was interesting that the out-of-water vibrations occurred at about the same rate as they did in the arm of a man lying on the same mattress. These microvibrations were also observed in other warm-blooded animals, but not in a snake, which is a cold-blooded animal.

What about the effect of immersion? In the first place, water conducts heat about 25 times more readily than air. So the faster a whale swims, the greater the cooling, because the water passes its body at a higher speed. The very fact of being immersed at temperatures considerably below that of the body makes greater demands on the "heating" system of the cetaceans, just as it does when you are immersed in water.

Whales cannot depend on shelter, or on hunching and curling up, to reduce heat loss, and they cannot take advantage of a breeze in a heat wave. Mostly they need protection against cold, and a whale's very shape—streamlined for smooth motion—is a protection against heat loss. The parts of your body that are most likely to feel the cold are the ones that stick out—your ears, nose, fingers, and toes. The whale's streamlined body and its thick layer of insulating blubber conserve body heat and prevent rapid cooling by the icy ocean waters. On the other hand, it still has the large thin fins and flukes through which heat must be lost, as it is from our fingers and toes.

If an insulating blanket is too thick, it can interfere so much with heat loss that the animal actually gets hot and might even die of heat stroke. The blubber insulation can actually cause charring of the flesh underneath it; this has been seen in whales that have been dead for several days.

A factory ship (from a mural in the Chicago Natural History Museum)

When a factory ship is operating at sea, it is a common practice to tie up one whale to the side of the ship as a fender against bumping by the catcher vessels. If it is allowed to remain too long before being hoisted on deck and flensed, the tissues underneath the blubber become steaming hot, and the flesh may even be charred. This is because even in the ice-cold polar seas, the carcass begins to decompose from within by bacterial action. The heat generated by the bacteria is so great that the meat is burned "to a crisp."

The living whale, on the other hand, does not overheat, because the blubber is a living blanket: it grows thick, or thins out, under certain conditions. It is thicker in the Greenland whale that lives in the Arctic Ocean, and thinnest in the Bryde's whale, found mostly in warm tropical seas. Also, it is not equally thick over all parts of a whale's body. And its thickness varies with the season of the year.

For example, in our fall (southern summer) the rorquals migrate to the Antarctic, where they find krill aplenty. During this Antarctic season—up to about the end of January—these whales store up a great amount of fat, and this is laid down first in the blubber. When the blubber reaches a certain thickness (and this varies from 5 to 10 inches, depending upon the type of whale), the fat is then stored to a lesser extent in the blubber, and more in the bones and other tissues.

At the end of the season, when the whale returns to warmer waters, the blubber begins to thin out, and continues to become thinner during the "lean" months when it eats very little or not at all: the whale is calling upon its reserve stores of fat. To make up for the greater loss of heat, it swims more actively, the way you help keep yourself warm on a cold day by jumping up and down or swinging your arms.

There are other times when the whale's blubber undergoes changes in thickness. In the female, the blubber is thickest during pregnancy, and thinnest when it is nursing the infant whale. While it is carrying the developing fetus, it gains weight by storing up fat. Later, when the growing whale is suckling, the mother's body fat is reduced by the production of fat-rich milk.

The blubber is thickest on the back and hind parts of the body. It is thin around the blowhole, the eyes, the lower lip, the dorsal fin, and the flippers, and thinnest around the fluke. We can only guess that since these parts are active they deposit less fat than the flanks, for example. (In man there is less fat in the fingers than in the abdomen.) But whatever the reason, the whale's fluke is the most important part of its body for heat regulation. It has been called a heat exchanger.

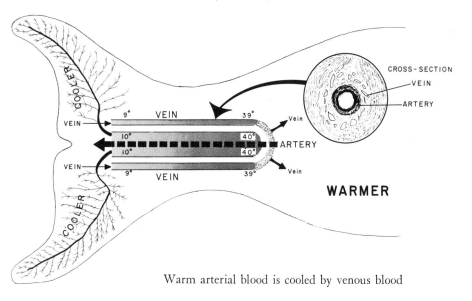

Warm arterial blood is cooled by venous blood

Whales caught after a long hunt bleed more freely from the tail than when they are killed quickly. When a dolphin is very active, the temperature of its flukes is much higher than that of the rest of its surface. This makes possible more rapid conduction of heat from the body. On the other hand, the flukes may also be much cooler than the rest of the body, serving as heat conservers. This dual function is linked to a special arrangement of the blood vessels in the flukes, as well as in the fins.

Because they have the thinnest blubber, the fins and the flukes can act like pumps, drawing the heat from the rest of the body. Here it has been found that the arteries are surrounded by special veins or by a whole network of thin-walled veins. Since the warm blood coming from the arteries is, by this arrangement, in close contact with the cooler blood returning in the veins, heat exchange takes place: the warm arterial blood is cooled by the venous blood which, in turn, has been chilled in the flukes. The result is a steep drop of temperature from the body toward the appendage. The heat of the arterial blood does not reach the flukes, but is shunted back into the body through the veins. Therefore, by keeping the fins and flukes cold, the body heat is conserved. On the other hand, when dolphins become over-heated for some reason, the flukes become markedly warmer than the rest of the body surface. In this way the body is cooled by losing excess heat from the flukes.

This special system, peculiar to cetaceans, tends to minimize sudden changes in body temperature. You can compare this ar-rangement to a vestibule, or a revolving door, or double-doored entrance to a house. In winter, an outer door will prevent the escape of heat from the main part of the house; in summer, the outer door is taken off to reduce the insulating effect of station-ary air in the enclosure.

The skin over the rest of the whale's body is also involved in heat regulation. But over the millions of years since the an-cestors of modern whales abandoned the land, their skin has undergone certain changes: whales have no sweat glands, no oil glands, and no fur. But there are changes also in the skin's circulation.

Whale skin, like ours, is made up of two layers, an outer *epidermis* and an inner *dermis*. In whales, as in humans, finger-like projections called *papillae* extend from the dermis into the epidermis. In the whale these papillae reach far up into the epi-dermis, but there are about half as many of them per square inch as in man. A tiny artery enters each papilla, branching into a network of capillaries at its tip. Completely surrounding each little artery is a network of veins, similar to those around the larger blood vessels in the flukes. Such an arrangement is also found in the gums of baleen whales. All three of these regions are in close contact with cold water, which would cause the blood to be readily cooled, were it not for the way the venous network envelops each small artery. This special set of veins helps to retain the heat of the body. Also, since there are fewer papillae in whale skin, there are also fewer capillaries and there-fore less blood to be cooled. A second set of veins winds around

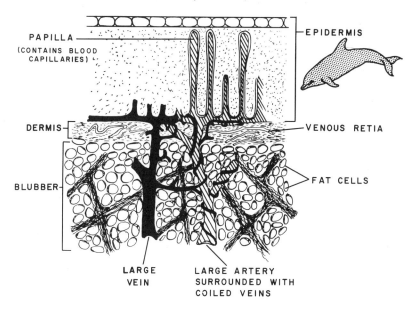

PAPILLA
(CONTAINS BLOOD CAPILLARIES)

EPIDERMIS

DERMIS

VENOUS RETIA

BLUBBER

FAT CELLS

LARGE VEIN

LARGE ARTERY SURROUNDED WITH COILED VEINS

Diagram of microscopic view of porpoise skin

the small arteries in the dermis as ivy winds around a tree trunk. This entwining of the small arteries is a means of diverting the blood whenever heat is to be preserved. On the other hand, when there is excessive heat production, as during fast swimming, this second circulatory pathway is detoured through larger veins in the blubber. The blood then flows more freely, without cooling, through the small arteries and therefore with greater heat loss, through the surface capillaries. So while the whale relies mainly on its flukes for getting rid of excess heat, its skin is chiefly a heat-conserving organ.

With the successful capture and tanking of dolphins, it was found that overheating of these animals is an actual possibility, and that the moist skin may play a vital part in the regulation of body temperature. When the animals were removed from the water and transported to an inland aquarium, their bodies over-

Transporting a whale out of water. Marineland staff members have flown whales from California to Florida, keeping them out of water for as long as 50 hours

heated by about 10 degrees, and they died. It was soon learned that during such excursions out of the water the skin must be kept continually moist by constant hosing down with cold water or with wet wrappings.

The complicated adjustments that whales, like other mammals, have to make, in order to maintain a steady temperature, are partly controlled by the central nervous system and partly by endocrine glands. The size of blood vessels and the accompanying shifts in blood supply are controlled by nerves whose activity is determined by centers in the brain and spinal cord. The chief heat regulating center is located in the base of the brain, called the *hypothalamus.* Heat production is controlled mainly by endocrine glands, and the most important of these is the thyroid gland.

The whale's thyroid gland is proportionately larger than in comparable land animals. In a beluga whale and a horse, both weighing exactly 1,048 pounds—the thyroid gland of the whale weighed $3\frac{1}{2}$ ounces, the horse's $1\frac{1}{6}$ ounces. This same ratio was found when porpoises were compared with land-dwelling mammals of the same size, such as calves.

These figures seem to show that the whale has a high metabolism (rate of oxidation) because its larger thyroid gland secretes more thyroid hormone, *thyroxin,* and so stimulates its body to burn food at a faster rate. Terrestrial animals that make their home in the Arctic also have large thyroids which enable them to produce enough heat to compensate for the large heat losses at low temperatures.

While the thyroid in whales is relatively large, the adrenals —two small glands tucked in between the diaphragm and the front of the kidneys—are relatively small. And they are smaller in the rorquals than in dolphins and porpoises. In other mammals, the adrenals also decrease in relative weight with body weight. Still, the small adrenals in cetaceans have special significance apart from relationship to body size. When these glands were compared in a beluga whale and a thoroughbred racehorse of the same weight, the horse was found to have larger adrenals. Cats and tigers—animals that lie in wait for hours ready to pounce suddenly on their prey—also have large adrenals. This is explained when you know the function of the adrenals: their inner core, known as the *medulla,* produces the hormone *adrenalin.* When sudden spurts of energy are required, the medulla quickly discharges more of this hormone into the blood.

The racehorse, cat, and tiger have this in common: they are "sprinters," jumping into action on short notice. In this they are aided by the greater activity of their adrenals. Cetaceans, on the other hand, are not so much called upon to spring into action promptly as to remain steadily active for long periods of time in water in cold climates. Compared with terrestrial animals in temperate climates, they are "stayers." In their environment, the whales' large thyroid takes care of their needs for a high rate of metabolism, especially in the smaller whales with a relatively larger surface area and higher metabolism.

8

The Private Life of a Whale

CAN YOU IMAGINE anyone or anything keeping its sex a secret from expert scientist observers? The celebrated gentle killer, Moby Doll, caught in Vancouver in 1964, did!

For 85 days it was nursed, worried over, coaxed to eat, admired by the townspeople, visited and exclaimed over by notables of the entire world. Its voice was recorded, and even its intelligence was tested by whale scientists. And all the while its sex was mistaken! When the captive arrived in Vancouver harbor, a medical team was on hand to take over. The physician-chief of the team was certain that the whale was a female, which is why it was named Moby Doll. Some weren't quite so sure of the whale's sex, and they dubbed it Moby Maybe. Much was learned about whale behavior during Moby "Doll's" three months' stay in its improvised sea-pen. But not all, for as David MacDonald wrote in *Rod & Gun* after the autopsy, "In death, the pleasantly surprising killer revealed one parting surprise: it was really a two-year-old male."

The fact that in whales the sexes are so difficult to distinguish is another of their many adaptations to aquatic life. Perfect streamlining requires a minimum of protruding body parts, and so the sex organs in both male and female are concealed within their body cavities. The mammary glands are also hidden, in a skin fold, and other secondary sex characteristics, such as the horns, antlers, beards, voice, and plumage that differentiate male from female among terrestrial mammals and birds, are absent in cetaceans. Except for the difference in size—and they are both so huge that this is not easy to tell unless they

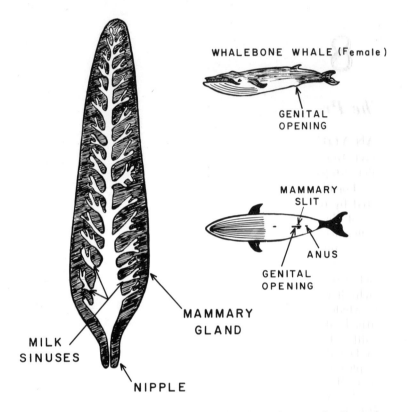

WHALEBONE WHALE (Female)

GENITAL
OPENING

MAMMARY
SLIT

ANUS

GENITAL
OPENING

MAMMARY
GLAND

MILK
SINUSES

NIPPLE

are seen together—there is little to differentiate male from female. Furthermore, there are exceptions to any rule you try to
make. The female blue whale is larger than the male, but the
male sperm whale is larger than the female.

If you want to tell the sex of a dolphin while you are watching it swim past an aquarium porthole or in a glass-walled tank,
you have to wait until it rolls over onto its back. First you must
know that in both male and female there is a circular anal opening, or vent, at the junction of the body and the peduncle of the
tail; the umbilicus is just about at the middle of the abdomen.
But the male has a single abdominal fold—nearer to the umbilicus than to the anus—which contains both the penis and a

slit to the exterior of the body, while the female has two slits, about five inches long, on each side of a longer midline slit (the genital opening). Each of the two side slits hides a small teat (nipple) connected with the milk glands.

Knowing all this, it's still not easy to tell the difference. When people who work with dolphins say they can easily tell the difference, it may be that, like mothers of twins, they can tell them apart because of other differences familiar to them.

However, it apparently is easier to distinguish male from female pilot whales. Dr. Henry Kritzler writes about one species —*Globicephala macrorhyncha:*

> The immature males resembled the female in body form. The adult males, . . . could easily be distinguished by the bulbous nasal protuberance which overhangs the tip of the snout only in that sex, by the prominent hump from just behind the blowhole to the base of the dorsal fin, by the great size of the dorsal fin and by the considerably more attenuated appearance of the pectoral fins and flukes.

Perhaps this will help you identify a male pilot whale if you visit one in an aquarium. (See picture on page 146.)

Underside view of female rorqual

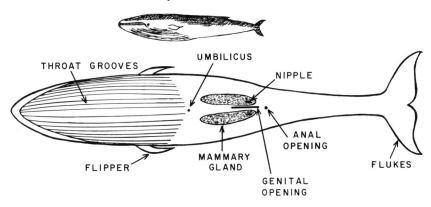

Underside of North Atlantic Pilot whale showing genital and mammary slits

Everything we know about reproduction in whales has had to be pieced together, mainly from two sources: examination of carcasses on whaling ships and in whaling stations, and observations of living dolphins in aquaria. In both places, attempts are constantly being made to find answers.

Of interest are the questions whalers themselves keep asking. How often and how many young does the female bear? How can we tell the age of a whale? What is a whale's lifespan? What is its age at sexual maturity? How often is the female in season or "in heat"? Where and when do whales mate? How long is it from impregnation to birth in the different kinds of whales? And (since about half of the sexually mature females killed are pregnant) how can we recognize a pregnant female at sea?

Biologists also are at sea when it comes to knowing about the actual birth process in the great whales. What causes difficult labor in some whales, often resulting in stillbirths? What about twins, family life, and care of the young? And what makes the newborn calf surface for its first breath?

Extensive studies at whaling stations from the northern shores of Norway to the Antarctic, on the island of South Georgia, from Japan to British Columbia—have given us answers to many questions, but many others remain unanswered. For example, Dr. Slijper tells us that no one has ever witnessed the birth of a rorqual, and so all that is known about the large whales and birth is based on examination of only three females, who died in labor. This may seem astonishing when you think of the thousands of whales taken every year, and of the many others whalers have observed but failed to capture. (One problem is that most whales give birth out of the usual capture season.) Also—and this is the important point—unlike seals, sea-lions and sea-otters, *whales give birth under water*. Migrating from the poles to the equator, they show little more than their heads and backs to the observer, "hiding the secret of their intimate life under a screen of sea," as Dr. Slijper so aptly puts it.

On the other hand, a great deal has been learned recently by direct observations of birth in the one species that is being studied intensively—the bottlenose dolphin (*Tursiops truncatus*). Their "private life" is no longer private, for marine biologists have studied dolphin mothers during pregnancy and labor, have seen and felt the movements of the fetus through the mother's belly wall, and have followed the young dolphin every step of the way from birth and nursing care to adulthood and parenthood. Before the problems of rearing the bottlenose in captivity had been solved, the only observation of a porpoise giving birth in a tank was at the Brighton Aquarium in England, in 1914—but the infant was stillborn. It was not until years later, on February 26, 1947, that an infant whale, born in captivity, lived—at Marine Studios, Marineland, Florida.

The mother, a performing bottlenose dolphin named Mona, gave birth to a daughter christened Spray. Spray thrived under the conditions of tank life, and seven years later brought forth a healthy baby of her own. Spray's mother went on to have other children, so there is now information about the length of pregnancy in dolphins and about the intervals between successive births. Babies have since been born to other mothers at Marineland and elsewhere in Florida and California. But when Spray became a mother, she provided the first definite proof of the length of time it takes for a young dolphin to reach child-bearing age.

By self-imposed regulations of the whaling industry, every captured female must be carefully examined for the presence of an embryo. Since the season lasts from 4 to 6 months, pregnant females are seen at varying stages of the development of the fetus, so incidental to learning facts of commercial importance, whaling inspectors have been able to study the reproductive systems of both sexes, and to learn about other questions, such as twinning.

In the main, both the male and female genital organs resemble those of other mammals, with only the modifications imposed by aquatic life. For example, the testes in most mammals are found in an external pouch; in cetaceans they lie inside, on each side of the kidneys. But apart from their position inside the body, the testes and the *epididymis* (the coiled tube attached to the upper part of each testis) are shaped and structured like those in other mammals. And although the blue whale's testes may weigh up to 100 pounds, their *spermatozoa* (male sex cells)

Inside view of male porpoise showing sexual organs

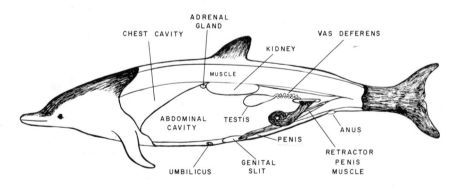

are no larger than man's, and reach the urethra, inside the penis, in a similar glandular secretion, the *semen*. But while in man several glands contribute to the semen, in whales the only additional structure is the prostate gland.

The whale's penis is attached to the pelvic bone in the abdominal cavity. It is coiled into an S-shape, its upper end held in place by a pair of strap-like retractor muscles, while the lower end is surrounded by a fold of abdominal skin behind the genital slit. During sexual activity, the retractor muscles slacken and the penis is thrust out through this slit. In many terrestrial mammals the penis becomes hard and erect through the inflow of blood into a meshwork of blood-containing spaces; in cetaceans erection of the male sex organ is due not to the sudden rushing of blood but to the elasticity of its particularly tough connective tissue; also the penis is extruded by muscular action. This type of structure seems to be designed for rapid copulation, as in dolphins, and whalers have occasionally reported that from their observations it is also rapid in the larger whales. This structural feature of the whale penis is also seen in other animals which copulate quickly, such as bulls, rams, and stags.

In the female cetacean the ovaries are roughly in the same place in the lower abdomen as are the testes in the male. The ovaries contain grape-like bumps called follicles, each follicle housing a single *ovum* or egg cell. When the sexually mature female is in heat (in whales as in many other animals this coincides with the mating season) one follicle, matured or ripened, bursts and releases the ovum into the oviduct, a process called ovulation.

If the ovum is fertilized by a spermatozoon, the ruptured follicle is replaced by the *corpus luteum*, or yellow body, a large hormone-producing mass. The corpus luteum persists throughout pregnancy, since its hormone is necessary for the continued attachment of the embryo to the uterine wall. Whether or not ovulation is followed by a pregnancy, the corpus luteum eventually shrinks, leaving behind it the *corpus albicans*, or white body. This

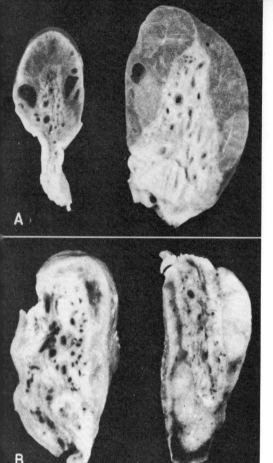

Corpora albicantia in a young, nursing female (a), and an old female (b)

functionless body, which is nothing more than the scar left by a once-active follicle, persists only in whales. Biologists have taken advantage of this fact in attempting to estimate the age of the whale.

The ovum travels down the oviduct to the uterus and, if fertilized, it becomes attached to the uterine wall. Here the embryo grows, getting its nourishment from the mother.

Like the spermatozoon, the whale ovum is no larger than the human ovum—100 to 200 microns. (A micron is $\frac{1}{25,000}$ inch.) From this tiny speck develops the 100-ton blue-whale colossus, 24 feet long at birth and weighing nearly three tons.

Sometimes more than one follicle matures in a season, but as a rule one liberated ovum is fertilized—and since fertilization, once the ovum is discharged, is usual in animals in their natural habitat—one calf is born. Whales produce only one calf in a single pregnancy, but twins, triplets, and even larger litters—up to sextuplets—are thought possible if more than one follicle ripens. Or, if the fertilized egg divides, twinning from the same egg is believed to occur once in three times. This idea is based on the number of embryos found in carcasses; but as yet there is no way of knowing whether all, or even more than one, would have developed into live babies. And during both pregnancy and nursing few other follicles reach maturity.

The vagina or birth canal is similar to that in land mammals except for the fact that it is lined by a series of folds. The exact function of these folds is not known, but they are believed to keep water out of the uterus and to enlarge the birth canal by unfolding during birth. Another feature—different from the human—is the division of the uterus, for part of its length, into two horns. The fertilized ovum develops in one horn only, and a rather strange and as yet unexplained finding is that in all toothed whales so far studied the embryo almost invariably becomes attached to the left horn, while in baleen whales the fetus may develop in either, but more frequently in the right horn. (See picture on page 150.)

The life history of the whale is very important to whalers. For example, where and when whales mate has a vital bearing on their conservation, perhaps making the difference between killing off the species and allowing it to multiply. A case in point is the history of the California gray whale during the past century.

From their feeding grounds in the North Pacific, the Bering Sea, and the Chuckchi Sea they swam southward off the coasts of British Columbia and the northern United States every December as regularly as the swallows come to Capistrano.

Whole ovary of an old Pilot whale showing thirteen corpora albicantia

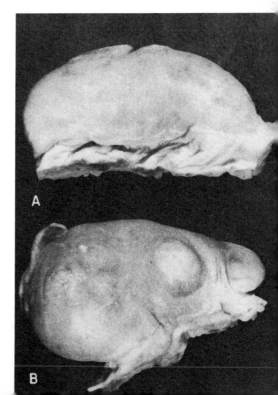

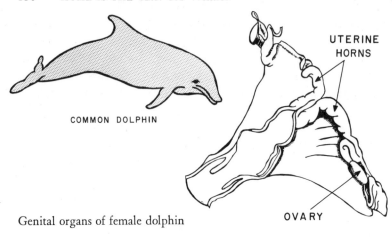

COMMON DOLPHIN

UTERINE
HORNS

OVARY

Genital organs of female dolphin

They were on their way to warm waters, some to give birth to their young, others to mate in the Mexican lagoons around Baja California. Then, from March to May, they all returned to their northern home, often staying close to shore and swimming through seaweed. Or, they have been known to congregate in great masses off Vancouver Island before disappearing into the Northern Pacific.

Early in the nineteenth century, the West Coast Indians looked for their arrival and hunted them for meat. Then the whales seem to have disappeared. Did they go far out to sea to avoid the harpoons? At any rate, they were not seen again until 1854. Their "reappearance" is one of the strangest stories in whaling history. And when they did reappear, one New England whaler and his crew kept it a tight secret for several years.

At that time whalers were still shipping out of New Bedford, Massachusetts, sailing southward, rounding stormy Cape Horn, and returning only after they had filled their barrels with whale oil, even if it took two, three, or four years. But, according to Roy Chapman Andrews, one among them returned with a full cargo after a few months. This was Captain Charles Scammon in his square rigger, the *Boston*. No one knew the secret of his success, but many were determined to find out—and did.

It seems that one winter Captain Scammon's catcher boats were chasing whales along southern shores of California when suddenly the whales disappeared. The captain, bent on finding out where the animals had vanished to, explored the shore until he discovered a narrow channel of deep water that led into a lagoon (since named Scammon's lagoon). He followed it for some miles, nearly to the edge of the desert, where he came upon a find that whalers imagine only in their dreams: thousands of whales, many of them with newborn calves.

For several seasons his men ruthlessly slaughtered the whales, but not without encountering the fury of the animals fighting for their young. Many of the sailors lost their lives and others returned with broken bones, but they went on killing what they called "devilfish" (because of the whales' savage defense of their young) for their share in the handsome profits. And of course they tried to keep it a secret. But the other whalers were determined to crack it.

One night they followed Scammon and, just as the whales disappeared, his ship slipped out of sight into the lagoon. The other whalers were mystified, but did not give up. And then one night, when the wind was right, the crew of a whaling ship smelled a familiar odor: steaming blubber. Sure enough, from their lookout they spied the masts of Scammon's ship and the secret was no more.

This was the beginning of the end of the gray whales, or so it seemed. After seasons of indiscriminate killing, the number of gray whales was tremendously reduced to the point where it was no longer profitable to hunt them, and the ships went elsewhere. Between the 1870's and early 1920's whaling off the coast of California ceased altogether. Then, in the winter of 1912, gray whales were sighted in the Sea of Japan, off the east coast of Korea, by Roy Chapman Andrews, the renowned explorer and whale expert. Reporting in 1954 on his adventure, Andrews wrote:

When I was in Japan in 1910, I learned of a whale called the *Koku Kujira* (devil whale). It appeared along the coast of Korea in the winter, traveling southward close inshore. Its description and habits sounded like Scammon's description of the lost California gray whale. But I could hardly believe it. The gray whale was extinct! I might just as well think about rediscovering a dinosaur!

Andrews examined a great many of these whales caught during their southward migration, and they seemed to him to be identical to those once so plentiful in the lagoons of southern California.

Today there are two populations of gray whales, Korean and Californian. Both live in the Northern Pacific near the Arctic Circle, the former in the Sea of Okhotsk off the coast of Kamchatka, the latter in the Bering Straits. During the summer both fatten up mainly on the small euphausia shrimp and bottom-dwelling crustacea abundant in the polar waters, and it is possible that they interbreed.

After the dramatic comeback early in the century, gray whales began to return in larger numbers to the Mexican lagoons. But again in the late 1920's and 1930's they were "overfished"—this time more efficiently, by explosive harpoons fired from cannons on whaling factory ships—so they came to the brink of a second "extinction." By 1935 or so there were probably no more than 100 of these hardy animals left. Then in 1937, by international agreement, the California gray was put under protection against all hunting. Today they are back by the thousands.

In the late autumn, when the days shorten, they begin their 6,000 mile trek down our Pacific coast. It is not known why they stay close to shore. It may be that they are probing for the entrance to their breeding place, but every winter they turn up in their ancient accustomed breeding grounds. First come the pregnant females, usually early in December, to relieve themselves of their 12- to 14-foot calves; then in January come other females, followed by the males, for the mating season. In March and April, with almost no rest and much thinner than when they arrived, they set forth again on the return journey to the Arctic. Each winter this giant parade brings thousands of visitors, who go out in excursion boats about a mile off shore to witness this great drama. Others watch it from the summit of Point Loma on San Diego Bay, where there is a Public Whale Watch sponsored by the National Park Service.

To study their rate of increase, scientists have established two censuses, one taken from the air, the other from land. The cooperating census takers are the Scripps Institution of Oceanography and the National Fish and Wildlife Service. The air census counts the adults and calves in the breeding grounds; the land census is taken as the migrating adults pass Point Loma. It is estimated that together they account for about one-half to one-third of the total population.

The important point is that there has been a steady rise in the gray whale population: from December 1946 to February 1947, 200 were counted; in the 1953 season there were 1,156; in 1954, 1,400; and during the 1964–65 migration, 6,000 were expected, but not nearly that many came.

In 1955, it was estimated by Dr. Raymond M. Gilmore, a research biologist of the Fish and Wildlife Service, that "the present breeding grounds of the gray whale could accommodate a population of about 25,000. . . ." However this depends upon the nations involved in the agreement, and while the moral of the gray whale story can hardly be ignored by the whalers, it remains to be seen whether they will take it to heart. Some scientists feel that they will not.

The mating season varies for different whale species, and every month of the year is on the mating calendar for one or another type somewhere in the world. Most whales mate in

Fetus of a Sei whale

warm waters to which migrating species travel from their regular feeding grounds, the northern species mating in early spring. The southern species migrate to the tropics for breeding. They probably mate immediately after their arrival in the tropics when their reserves are still large. Both sexes are better prepared for breeding after the body reserves have been built up. The males expend a great deal of energy during mating, and the females while nursing, so the migrations seem to be important both in obtaining food and in the successful carrying out of the reproductive function.

But not all species migrate. Bryde's whale, a rorqual resembling the sei and found exclusively in the tropics and sub-tropics, is probably in season all year round, fulfilling the functions of bearing and feeding the young without migration. The narwhal, an Arctic inhabitant, and the killer, found in all seas, do not migrate, and are thought to be in season the year round.

The sperm whale, with three distinct homes—the southern

hemisphere, the North Atlantic and the North Pacific—breeds at different times, depending on where it lives. Those in the southern hemisphere have their mating season late in our fall (spring in the southern hemisphere); the other two mate in the spring.

Whalers also want to know how often a particular species produces young. This depends upon a number of things: duration of pregnancy, how long the calf is nursed and, to some extent, as we have already learned about the blue whale, on the availability of food. In warm weather, in the wake of the retreating ice, the whales migrate to the Antarctic where the plankton grows luxuriantly. After months of feeding to the full, they return to temperate waters for mating. (Remember that the newborn calf has only a thin insulation of blubber and would probably freeze to death if born in icy waters.) Clearly, the migration habits are adapted to the biological needs of the animal.

Except for those that do not migrate over large distances, and whose calves may be born at any time of the year, most whales give birth about every two years, carrying their young about 11 months and, except for the rorquals, nursing for another 12 months. Sperm whales give birth only once in three years. Partly this is because they have a longer pregnancy; but it could be also because their food supply is not as certain as that of the krill eaters. About this, we can only speculate.

Humpback whale (*Megaptera novaengliae*)

Even whales that nurse for less than 12 months apparently have no more than one pregnancy in two years. This is true even of the large rorquals, which do not nurse as long as the toothed whales, and for the gray, blue, and fin whales the nursing periods are respectively 5, 7, and 6 months. The only rorqual that nurses for nearly a year is the humpback. (See picture on page 155.)

How many young does a whale produce in its lifetime? We would expect that to depend, first, upon the age at sexual maturity and second—assuming that it breeds to the end of its life— upon its lifespan. From biological researches on whales, estimates are now available for both these ages for the better-known species. Both males and females become sexually mature at the same age in a given species, and for most this is probably when they are between 4 and 6 years of age. Notable exceptions are the common porpoise and the female beluga, which are thought to reach sexual maturity at about half that age.

The lifespan is difficult to know for most species that live in the wild, including whales. It has been estimated that whales live from 20 to 30 years (Greenland whales may live 40 years). Biologists are still working on more accurate gauges of length of life as well as of the number of offspring for each cow.

Whale experts have counted the number of *corpora albicantia*—the scars of ruptured follicles. However, one would have to assume that each represents one pregnancy, but because it is not certain that pregnancy always follows ovulation, the scientists' count may be high in a given specimen. The present estimate is 8 to 12 young for most whales, with a possible high of 15 for the killers, belugas, and humpbacks. It may be possible to get exact information—at least for dolphins in captivity—when these have been followed through the natural lifetime of a population in an actively reproducing colony such as Marineland. The current guess is that their lifespan may not be long because of the high level of metabolism of these animals.

Meanwhile, other guesses were based on the counts of the

ovarian white bodies until, in 1940, Norwegian and Russian scientists independently found another basis: the annual growth zones in the baleen plates. By their method, the whale's age at sexual maturity, once believed to be two years, was "corrected" to four years. But the method also has its inaccuracies: the whale continually wears down its plates.

What some think to be a still more reliable determination was found during the 1955–56 whaling hunts. The ear tube of the baleen whales is filled with a wax-like plug which may somehow be involved in conducting sound from the outer opening to the inner ear. This plug continues to grow with the skull and shows alternating dark and light layers, considered to be distinct yearly growth zones, like the annual rings in a tree trunk, and the scales of fishes. In 1961, Dr. Alex Comfort, a British authority on biological aging, wrote that as yet there were too few specimens collected to test the accuracy of this method. Meanwhile, many thousands have been collected but, as Dr. Slijper pointed out in a note to the authors, the trouble is that no ear plug is known from a whale whose exact age has been determined.

Far more is known about the rate of growth of the young whale than about the age of its parents. A blue whale, weighing close to 3 tons at birth, grows to 23 tons at weaning (at about 7 months of age). At this rate, during its infancy it gains 200 pounds a day and grows to more than twice its birth length of 24 feet. Compare this rate of growth with a human baby, which at birth averages from 19 to 21 inches, and at 7 months is about 27 or 28 inches long.

Of course, the growth rate of the whale slows down after weaning, as soon as it is on its own and feeding on krill. Still, it is estimated that it gains at the rate of 90 pounds daily for 4 years, when it reaches adult size.

The amazing growth during the whale's nursing period is due to the rich milk it gets from its mother. Cow's milk and human milk contain about 88 per cent water; whale milk has only 40 to 50 per cent water. Thick and creamy, it contains about 40 per cent fat, 11 or 12 per cent protein, 1 or 2 per cent lactose (milk sugar) and 1 per cent salts and vitamins. Whale milk is from three to four times as concentrated as that of most domestic animals—cows and goats, for example. Contrast it also with human milk with its 6 per cent milk sugar, from 1 to 2 per cent protein, and about 4 per cent fat.

Just how much milk a whale produces and how much the calf takes at each feeding has so far been impossible to estimate with any degree of accuracy. Authorities' estimates differ, but 130 gallons a day is a rough one for the large whales. Since whales are believed to feed about 50 times a day, the calf must get about two-and-a-half gallons at each nursing. Considering that the nursing period lasts for only a few seconds, the calf of a large whale must get quite a jet of milk with each mouthful!

In 1947, the first dolphin was born alive and healthy in captivity. The information gained from this event about cetacean birth not only has eliminated much of the previous guesswork, but has verified some earlier speculations. Starting in 1951, a handful of scientists at Marineland, Florida, by patient and continual observation of living animals, have been able to piece together a remarkable story. They have published several papers, and after reading them it appears that little remains secret about the private life of the bottlenose dolphin.

Except for Spray, conceived in the wild before capture, all the others described in these papers were fathered in the tank in which they were born. During most of a year, Frank, the male dolphin, was seen to mingle freely with all others in the tank—males and females, adult and young. Then early in the spring he began showing a preference for the company of a particular female, remaining with her for long periods. He hovered over her and chased her when she left him. The courtship activities which followed were unmistakably different from anything that had

Courtship

occurred before he began paying attention to the female of his
choice. The observers describe such characteristic courting behavior as "posturing"—lifting his tail, stroking the female with
his flippers or patting her head lightly, nuzzling various parts of
her body, not unlike a human mother's nuzzling of her baby,
"mouthing" with open snout, jaw-clapping, and yelping. This
typical behavior (seen later in other dolphins) continued for
many days until the female responded in her own way, when it
was terminated by rapid copulation, resulting in the impregnation of the female. Immediately Frank lost interest and turned
his attention to other females, so from then on the observations
were centered on the expectant mother.

During most of her pregnancy the female behaves like other
dolphins in the tank—feeding, swimming, and playing as usual.
But in the final three or four months there are noticeable changes
in her appearance and behavior. The abdomen is greatly dis-
tended, showing in profile a pronounced swelling on the left side,
and the typical "step" above the caudal peduncle. Her navel all

Pigmy Sperm whale fetus (*Kogia breviceps*)

but disappears and, as the fetus grows, flickers of movement are seen on her abdomen and actually felt by divers as they gently stroke her side.

As term (birth time) approaches, the expectant mother tends to withdraw from her tank companions, and will swim against the current to avoid contact with them. One year two pregnant females were seen keeping close together, swimming at the outer rim of the tank. Because of a gap in their ages, these two had not been close companions before pregnancy, but now they acted as if they had discovered a common bond in anticipated motherhood. They engaged less in the usual spontaneous play, and became less interested in performing such tricks as playing "fetch" with objects thrown into the tank. One of them even permitted a newcomer, a young and emaciated captive, to attempt suckling at her nipple. Assuming the role of "foster parent," she "invariably slowed down when this happened, just as she would if she were nursing her own infant," the observers wrote. Both pregnant females protected the sickly foundling, but it soon died. Because no trace of milk was found in its stomach, it would seem that whale milk does not form in the mammary glands until after birth, which is also true of humans. This incident was cited by the authors as a sign that the mother dolphin "is psychologically prepared for the care of the young" before its birth.

The most dramatic event is the birth itself. The mother begins to swim about a great deal, apparently seeking a secluded spot. Her abdomen shows active contractions, the genital opening begins to distend and widen, and she makes frequent barking sounds not heard in the tank at other times. Within a few minutes the fetus begins to emerge—tail first.

Here we see a most striking difference between the whale and land mammals, such as the cow, which bear only one or two large and completely developed young. In the latter, as in humans, a normal birth begins with extrusion of the head, because otherwise—with a feet-first "breech presentation," the baby may not be born alive, and there will certainly be difficulties in delivery.

Lying folded toward the underside of the uterus, the flukes of the whale-to-be-born slip out just after the appearance of the stem of the peduncle. The mother's abdominal contractions continue while the baby's tail lies motionless for about half an hour

Baby dolphin being born, tail first (note mother's bulging "step")

Mother whale pushing stillborn infant up

after the beginning of labor, and the mother goes through violent spasms, her body bent and her flukes lifted, and after several powerful movements the baby slides out. Some births take as little as five minutes.

Then comes the final act of the drama: the separation of infant from mother. The mother whirls around in a sudden about-face, snapping the umbilical cord, and the baby is born! Within a few seconds after it is free, it surfaces. Only on surfacing does its blowhole open, when it takes its first breath, filling its lungs with air. If it fails to surface, the mother nudges it upward, assisted by another female who has been called an "aunty." And even after it has taken several breaths and is swimming, it is still shielded between the bodies of the mother and aunty.

Pushing the infant up to get its first breath is so much a part of the whale's instinctive behavior that mothers of dead babies have been seen to persist in this effort for hours. On one occasion, when a calf was born dead in Marineland, the mother was helped by all the females in the tank, who took turns—for four hours—pushing the dead infant to the surface.

Among the scores of cetacean adaptations to a life spent exclusively in the water there is none more extraordinary than its manner of birth—tail first. What is significant about the dolphins' determination to achieve tail-first birth? Would head-first extrusion be dangerous or even fatal for the offspring as feet-first extrusion may be for humans? The point is that in cetaceans the shape of the fetus, and of its mother's abdominal cavity, and such things as the center of gravity and length of umbilical cord make tail presentation the "normal" or adapted way for a whale to be born.

In some instances this position is attained only a few hours before birth, the fetus actually turning around in the uterus. A most interesting first-hand account was recently given by Frank S. Essapian of a head presentation by two dolphins in Florida's Marineland, believed to be the first such occurrences in captivity.

In the case of Mona, the labor was difficult and long-drawn out—nearly 12 hours—during which a bag-like rounded mass protruded and was finally withdrawn. The following day, after the mother was relaxed and quiet, the birth commenced again and the baby dolphin was born normally within 50 minutes after the beginning of labor. The explanation given by the observer was that "once the fetus had become properly oriented, Mona experienced no difficulty in completing the birth, which was carried out normally, and was of normal duration."

In the case of Mrs. Jones, a dolphin seen to have the same difficulty, the "protruding object" was the baby's beak (the fetal membrane having been broken) which was alternately pushed out and pulled back, each time within about a minute. Again this occurred during a prolonged labor, until "with the increased pressure exerted on the walls of the birth passage by the greater girth of the fetus," the baby was finally born during "one mighty contraction" that caused some damage to the mother.

Of extreme interest was the excitement these births created in the other dolphins in the tank. The volume of whistles and other sounds increased, and in each case the dolphin in labor was surrounded by females who seemed to try to help. They lifted one off the bottom with their beaks, and returned repeatedly to look closely at her underside. Even more unusual was the attention paid to Mrs. Jones by the bull, an attentiveness which carried over to the calf, as he did "baby sitting" for it while the mother went to feed at the platform. And when the calf was chased by a female, the bull joined Mrs. Jones in protecting the calf from the intruder.

How did dolphins "know" that these births were unusual, calling for special concern and care? It may be that they were responding to special distress calls of the mothers. Essapian suggests another reason, based on Mrs. Jones' infant appearing with the exposed snout: this meant that the protective membrane (the amnion) had been ruptured, releasing some of the amniotic fluid into the water, which may have been detected by her companions. He points out that the mass dolphin interest shown in Mrs. Jones, "when as if on a signal, they approached her to examine her underside, is most striking. There can be little doubt, but that the excitement and the sudden curiosity were triggered by a special stimulus." Although it is very likely that the amniotic fluid was the immediate cause, Essapian thought it reasonable that the recognition of the danger involved hearing, sight, taste, or a combination of all of these senses.

Still another cetacean adaptation to the sea is the delayed expulsion of the *placenta* or afterbirth. In dolphins—and probably in other cetaceans—it may occur as long as 10 hours after birth. No one is sure, but it is thought that if the placenta slipped out right after the baby dolphin, and before the umbilical cord is ruptured, it might interfere with the baby's surfacing. Dr. Slijper writes that occasionally the umbilical cord does fail to rupture, in which case it probably pulls the placenta behind it, and because of its weight the calf is prevented from coming up for air. During the summer months, in fact, when porpoises are born in the North Sea, newborn ones are often washed up on the coast, with placenta still attached to an unruptured cord. And so while it is by no means certain whether these animals choked to death or died from other causes, "it seems reasonable to assume—until the matter is investigated further—that choking was responsible for some of the deaths at least."

Finally, there is the age-old question, never satisfactorily answered: what makes the human newborn baby take its first breath and utter its first cry right after it is ushered into the outside world; and what makes the newborn dolphin surface for the first time?

Of course there are explanations. It is said that as the baby dolphin falls free into the water after leaving the warm body of its mother, the sudden cold causes it to surface, and that the dryness of the air striking the nostril when the dolphin reaches the surface causes the blowhole to open. Both of these reactions are believed to be controlled by nerves in the skin. But there may be other things that help to stimulate blowing—perhaps even an accompanying first sound, immediately after birth.

Many ancient myths and legends had to do with the birth of a dolphin. One of these told of the young having been tucked into a pocket of the mother during the night—the legend perhaps originating from an erroneous observation that the infant was sliding *in* rather than out of the mother's body during birth. Another mistaken belief was that newborn cetaceans were poor swimmers until the fins and flukes acquired their final rigidity; this was probably because these structures appeared to be soft and floppy, and therefore inefficient for some time after birth. Actually, the young do pretty well in swimming. In Greenland it was believed that the flukes of narwhals and belugas emerged several weeks before birth, and that during this time the fetus practiced swimming with its flukes, readying itself to leave its mother and swim on its own.

Compared with a kitten or a puppy that is sheltered and warmed by its mother, usually in a previously prepared nursery, the newborn dolphin is well prepared for independent life. It swims from birth, and despite the softness and floppiness of its fins and flukes, it keeps up with its mother, even if for some reason she has to step up her speed; to do this it needs only to beat its flukes more rapidly and to breathe more often. Within a few days, sometimes within a few hours, the dorsal fin becomes stiff and upright; and the muscles that move the flukes begin to grow stronger.

The newborn dolphin, which is about three feet long—more than a third of its mother's length—and weighs about 25 pounds, closely resembles the adult in most respects, but a few features are characteristic of infancy. It has a row of seven or eight stiff hairs, like a bristly mustache, on its upper jaw; these drop off usually before the infant is a month old, but sometimes they persist for long periods. Its head is proportionately large for its body, just as it is in the newborn of other animals. Its neck shows more plainly than the neck of the adult does. On each side it has vertical creases (without the typical adult gray pigment) that are part of the wrinkling of the fetal skin, but these disappear as the baby fattens. And at birth its teeth are hidden in the gums for about 6 weeks, when they begin to erupt.

Apart from these signs of immaturity, there are others showing the newborn dolphin's readiness for life outside its mother's body. Its eyes are open at birth, and apparently it has good vision. It is vocal from the moment it is born; escaping bubbles from its own and its mother's blowhole indicate mutual communication; and it must be able to hear, since it responds to its mother's whistling calls.

About an hour or so after birth, the infant begins searching for the mother's nipple, and soon takes nourishment. The mother usually rolls over on one side, and the infant suckles by grasping the nipple between the tip of its palate and its grooved tongue, forming a watertight seal. The mother's mammary glands pour

Baby dolphin nursing

their milk into large sinuses (spaces), from which she expels it
by contracting her abdominal muscles as soon as the baby grasps
the nipple, squirting the milk into its mouth (now and then a
small amount may escape if the baby's hold is not tight). This
is quite different from the suckling action of other mammals
which must actively work to draw the milk out of the gland—a
much slower and longer feeding process. In the dolphin each
suckling lasts but a few seconds, but the feedings are much more
frequent, as often as every 15 minutes in the early weeks. Here
we see an adaptation to underwater feeding and to the need for
frequent surfacing for air with no interruption of swimming.

Maternal care is of a very high order in cetaceans, both in

Mother porpoise, infant, and guardian ("aunt")

nature and in captivity. In the ocean the young stay close to the
mother who sometimes is accompanied by a protecting "aunt,"
the only cow the mother will allow near her calf. If the mother
dozes off for a few seconds, the calf seeks safety under her tail.
If the calf is attacked or endangered in any way, the mother will
fight savagely to protect her offspring. This used to be a necessity
in the days when whalers killed young and old alike. But under
today's whaling regulations, a cow accompanied by a calf may
not be gunned, and the inspectors on whaling ships see to it that
this rule is scrupulously observed.

In the feeding grounds, the young cetaceans may swim
away from their mothers to forage, but they are in constant
touch with the mother by their calls and echolocation, the latter

developing after several weeks. In Marineland, Florida, where many dolphins have been born, the bottlenoses swim around in the tank by themselves and chase after fish a few weeks after birth and while they are still nursing. Since the dolphins have no teeth, the fish get away, but long before it is weaned, at about 16 months of age, the mother begins to teach her youngster how to snatch and swallow fish by placing a fish or a piece of squid in its mouth. Sometimes there are difficulties with weaning: the calf may rid itself of the first fish it eats, and then the mother massages its belly with her snout.

The mother's concern for her young, even in the sheltered environment of a tank, is illustrated by a story told by Doctors Arthur F. McBride and Henry Kritzler about one of their experiences in Marineland. A baby dolphin was born in the receiving tank, which was equipped with a walkway over the gate at both ends.

When the infant was but 13 minutes old, it swam under one of these overpasses. The mother darted under and, with her snout, guided him back into the center opening. . . . Each time he was seen to approach one [of the walkways] the mother dipped under him and, rising, flipped him away from the apparent danger with her snout. Nor was he permitted by his mother to approach the tank wall, against which he collided just once, when he was but a few minutes old.

Another story proves that such care is not misplaced. A female dolphin, born and raised at Marineland, for some reason was neglected by its mother: she allowed it to stray, left it alone at feeding time, failed to remove it from contact with other occupants of the tank, and did not protect it from dangerous situations. The infant died at the age of 15 days.

9

The Sea Through Their Senses

A TRAINED BOTTLENOSE dolphin can jump more than 16 feet above water and grab a baton from the end of a pole. It can snatch a cigarette from the mouth of its trainer who is standing on a platform 20 feet high. It can slip a basketball through a basket, leap through a hoop, and back up to catch a football in mid-air. Obviously, this species of dolphin must have remarkably good vision.

The experts tell us that whales, like land animals, vary widely in their ability to see, from the keen-eyed sea dolphins and porpoises to the totally blind Gangetic river dolphin. The gradations in keenness of vision, size of visual field, perception of depth and distance, and ability to see both in and out of the water, seem to be related mainly to where the animal feeds and what it eats. For example, dolphins feeding on fast-swimming fish fairly near the surface have good vision; pilot whales (primarily nocturnal animals in their natural habitat) and sperm whales (deep divers), both feed on slower-moving squid and cuttlefish and have small eyes and poor vision.

But regardless of how well or poorly they can see, the eyes of all cetaceans are fitted for life in the water. First of all their protective structures differ from those of land animals. Whales have no need for eyelashes to keep out dust, nor brows to prevent sweat from running into their eyes, nor, for that matter, for tear glands. If you get a speck of dust in your eye, it is usually washed out by an extra amount of secretion (tears) produced by the lacrimal glands; the overflow runs through the tear ducts into the nose. A whale has no lacrimal ducts or glands, and cannot weep.

After all, it doesn't have to "worry" about dust in the ocean. On the other hand, its eyes are better protected against irritation by salt water.

Whales have glands in the corner of each eye—Harder's glands—that produce an oily secretion which coats the eye surface and protects the *cornea*—the transparent window in front of the eyeball—from the harmful effects of constant exposure to seawater. Any excess oil is washed away by the sea, without having to drain into special ducts. The interesting thing is that such ducts have been found in the skulls of *Archaeocetes,* primitive cetaceans; over millions of years these ducts have disappeared and are absent in modern whales.

In addition, the outer part of the cornea and the *conjunctiva,* the thin membrane that covers it and lines the eyelids, is thickened with horny material; this further reduces the stinging from the brine. Also in toothed whales in captivity a constant secretion of heavy mucus around the surface of the eyes has been noticed both above and below water. And, like those of land animals, their eyelids can open and shut, providing further protection against injury. Bottlenoses in aquaria are seen to shut their eyes during "cat-naps," and it must be assumed that with the same well-developed lid muscles they can also blink.

Another adaptation is the unusual thickness of the *sclera,* the tough outermost layer of the eyeball itself, which prevents compression of the eyeball under the high pressure in deep water. Since the rounded shape of the eyeball is necessary for the focussing of a sharp image and for maintaining the normal width of the visual field, this scleral thickness is an important structural modification.

The most remarkable adaptations, however, are seen in the "business end" of the eye, which make vision possible in both water and air. One reason why it is more difficult for us to see under water is that light rays are bent at the point of contact of the water with the air. Another reason why we would expect the vision of whales to be poor when submerged is the reduction in

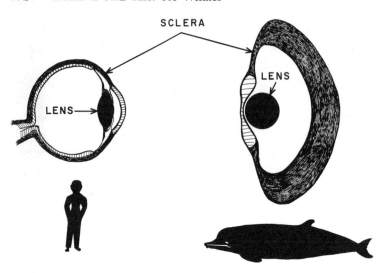

Sclera and lens of man and of whale

the amount of light penetrating the water. It has been estimated that nine-tenths of the light is absorbed at a depth of thirty feet, and of course whales dive deeper than that. So for a dolphin to be able to follow a fish at some depth and also to catch one thrown in the air, it must have some mechanism for adjusting to sight in these two different media.

The cetacean eye has a nearly spherical lens—the part that focusses the light rays on the retina—whereas our lenses are oval-shaped, adapted to bending light rays in air. The whale's spherical lens has the effect of a pair of thick convex glasses worn while under water by a man with normal vision. In other words, the whale's eye has greater light-bending power. Thus, man is far-sighted in water, the rays focussing behind the retina, while the whale is near-sighted in air, the rays focussing in front of the retina. Accordingly, without having to adjust the curvature of the lens under water, the image of a fish would focus on the whale's retina. Adjusted to seeing under water, is the whale really near-sighted in air and its image blurred? No one who has worked with bottlenose dolphins in aquaria doubts that they must see very well indeed to be able to sight targets in air as accurately as they do.

To be sure, scientists agree that toothed whales, including the sperm whale, have muscles that change the curvature of the lens, thereby accommodating for accurate vision. Baleen whales, on the other hand, lack such muscles and cannot see clearly above water. Under water they do not have to accommodate: the structure of the whale's eyes is especially adapted to the denser (water) medium. The lens is exceptionally rounded, the eyeball oval, making the distance between the lens and retina shorter than in land animals. This arrangement permits the light rays to focus on the retina without the need to adjust the curvature of the lens. In the less dense air medium, light rays would focus in front of the retina and produce a blurred image. Where food is concerned, the plankton eaters can do with less acute vision, since they need only open their jaws and get a giant mouthful of floating krill.

Another explanation has been suggested for whales seeing

Sight of man and dolphin in water and in air

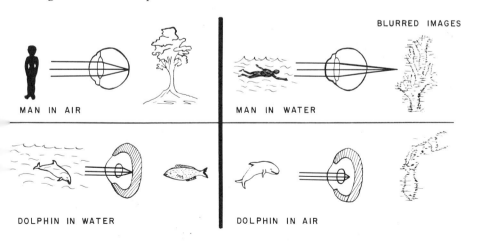

BLURRED IMAGES

MAN IN AIR

MAN IN WATER

DOLPHIN IN WATER

DOLPHIN IN AIR

both in and out of water. In all whales not only the lens but also the eyeballs are almost perfect spheres, but those of whales are more nearly ellipses—shorter from front to back and longer from top to bottom. It is also thought that the distance between the lens and the retina—equal at all points of our eyes—is greater in the upper than in the lower part of the whale eye. Since the image on the retina, as on a camera film, is formed upside down, an object in air would focus on the lower part of the retina (where the lens-to-retina distance is shorter), and an object in water would focus on the upper part of the retina where this distance is longer. This difference in the eye diameters could account for proper focussing of light on the retina both in and out of water. It has the same effect as if the whale put on concave lenses or bifocals to make up for its near-sightedness in air. Further work needs to be done to determine whether or not this is actually so.

Dr. John C. Lilly, referring to the "mystery as to how their [bottlenoses] vision can be so remarkable, both in water and in air," offers another possible explanation: "The extreme degree of accommodation may be achieved by a peculiarly shaped cornea: it may be shaped differently in the center than it is at the edges." But this, too, has to be established.

Since whales live in almost perpetual twilight, you would expect them to have the large eyes of night animals, such as the owl. Actually, their eyes are small for the size of their bodies. The question then arises: how do they manage to see with so little light reflected into the eye? It has been discovered that cetacean eyes, like those of cats, glow in the dark. Both contain iridescent crystals of a substance called *guanine* inside the *choroid* (the eye's pigmented layer), which includes the iris. These crystals give this layer a metallic appearance so that it reflects light as from a many-faceted mirror, enhancing vision in the dark.

How much and what part of its environment does the whale see, and can it judge distance as we do? Our eyes are situated in the front of the head. This means that the visual field—the part of our environment we can take in without moving the head—is 160 degrees—almost a half circle. Animals with their eyes placed on the side of the head have a much larger visual field. Rabbits, for example, have a visual field of 360 degrees, literally seeing all around—a fact of great importance to an animal constantly threatened from all sides. Actually they have two different visual fields: the right eye gets one picture and the left another. However, just because of this, their ability to judge depth and distance is sacrificed. Depth perception—stereoscopic vision—best developed in man and apes, is possible for the very reason that we get a single image due to an almost complete overlapping of the images on both retinas.

A few comparisons of the extent of overlapping of the visual fields in different animals show how the placement of the eyes in the head determines the degree of stereoscopic vision. In man, the stereoscopic field extends over 120 degrees, in the dog about 90, in the horse 60, and in the rabbit only 30 degrees. While hunted animals, with eyes placed on the sides, are aware of the hunter anywhere around them, man, like all hunting animals with eyes in front, can judge depth and, therefore, distance of his prey with great accuracy.

Offhand, you might think that cetacean eyes are not as well adapted to life as, for example, those of large birds. The eagle, a hunter with close-set eyes, swoops down on its quarry with utmost accuracy; a pilot whale refuses food placed in front of it, and accepts it only when it is moved to the side of its head. But what the whale loses in vision it gains in greater streamlining. If instead of small eyes on the sides of its head, it had large eyes in the front, its swimming speed would be reduced, and its eyes would meet continuous and severe friction from salt water. In other words, it is better adapted to fast locomotion than to keen sight.

It would be easy to fall into the serious error of concluding from this that the whale "has made its choice" and so has to live with it. The study of evolution teaches us, however, that certain structures either do or do not fit the organism to its environment and conditions of life. Over millions of years those features that have what the biologist calls survival value will become better developed with use, while those that are not helpful to survival will shrivel and disappear.

So you can see why dolphins with their small snouts and some degree of stereoscopic vision, as well as their greater head flexibility, enjoy better vision than the large *mysticetes* with almost rigid heads—particularly the sperm and pilot whales, whose blunt and bulbous heads almost completely obstruct their frontal view. On the other hand, Dr. Norris believes this is not true of the pilot whale.

Perhaps to make up for its second-rate vision, the whale's hearing is especially keen. As long as 2,500 years ago, Pindar, the ancient Greek lyrical poet, said that dolphins could be attracted by the tones of the flute and the lyre, and Aristotle marvelled at their rapid flight from all strange noises. They considered this all the more remarkable because they had not observed any ears in the animals; they didn't know that whales had openings to ears inside the head. (Not until the sixteenth century was the auditory passage in porpoises described, by Guillaume Rondelet, a French naturalist and student of marine life.)

The earliest hunters knew that whales could hear because they drove them into bays by beating the sides of their boats with wooden sticks, corralling them like cattle. And later, whalers hunting with steam-powered ships would throttle down the engines, so their prey wouldn't be startled by the noise, and head full speed for the open seas. To this day, people living on the Black Sea attract bottlenose dolphins with special whistles. And Johan T. Ruud, a marine biologist at the University of Oslo in Norway, noticed that when harpoons missed the target and merely fell into the water, the noise of the harpoon, itself, hitting the water caused the animals to get away, and fast. So many similar observations have been made that it seems that whales hear almost as well as bats.

But it is necessary to distinguish between hearing of noises produced in their environment and noises they make themselves. (You will read about this in the next chapter.) Both hearing and echolocation depend upon air or water vibrations (sound waves), but the vibrations involved in echolocation are usually so frequent or high pitched (they are largely supersonic or ultrasonic) that they cannot be heard by the human ear. Dogs can hear them, however, as you can tell if you use a dog whistle, and so can cetaceans.

The hearing organ of land mammals has three parts: the external ear, the middle ear, and the inner ear. Fish have only an inner ear, so they have to "hear" by bone conduction of sound waves; that is, through vibration of the skull bones. And when sound is perceived in this way, it is impossible to tell where it comes from—right or left, top or bottom, front or back. We detect the source of sound more accurately when the vibrations come mainly from one side.

The ear of a whale: (A) the ear plug and external auditory meatus in a baleen whale; (B) the absence of a plug in the external auditory meatus of a toothed whale. The inside of the middle ear—the bulla, petrous bone, and foam cavities—is about the same in both types

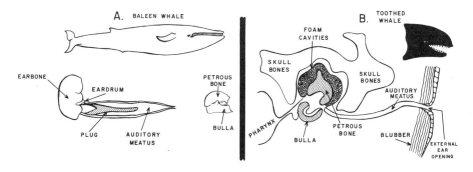

Until recently it was thought that whales, like fish, had no outer ear, could hear by bone conduction only, and so could not detect the direction or source of the sound. But we know now that whales have good directional hearing; the vibrations reach them through the middle ear—which is modified for hearing in water—and they have directional hearing because of a special feature not found in land mammals.

The whale has no visible *pinna*—the shell-shaped cartilagenous part of your external ear that you can see—but the cartilage has been found buried under the skin of cetaceans. The function of the pinna is to collect vibrations; it has small muscles by means of which some animals (rabbits, cats, horses) prick up and move their ears around to hear better. We have the same muscles—and some people can wiggle their ears for fun—but they are of no use to us because we turn our heads if we wish to pick up a sound more clearly. While the whale has no pinna like ours, a rudimentary one is seen in cetacean embryos, and certain muscles, attached to cartilage around the opening to the ear, are believed to be used in gauging depth or pressure—a function necessary for deep divers.

The other part of the external ear is the auditory *meatus,* the canal that conducts the air vibrations from the pinna to the tympanic membrane, the eardrum. The cetacean's meatus is a very narrow tube starting with a pinpoint opening in the skin just behind and below the eye. In toothed whales it is S-shaped and the same diameter throughout; in baleen whales it is funnelshaped, with the wider end inside, and closed in the center. The inner path is filled with a conical-shaped plug—the "wax plug"— which is not really wax at all but a horny material. (This is the structure that shows the annual rings by which scientists tell the age of baleen whales.) Most recent studies by British scientists show that this "wax plug" is also an excellent conductor of sound—especially the high tones inaudible to us, but which whales are known to hear well.

The human middle ear is a closed-in air cavity. It is

shut off from the meatus by the eardrum, a taut membrane that vibrates "in tune" with vibrations from the meatus. The inside or back wall of the middle ear is closed off by two additional and much smaller membranes, through which the vibrations are conducted to the inner ear. In the middle ear are three tiny bones called *ossicles;* these magnify the vibrations by thirty times, and transmit them to the inner ear.

The cetacean middle and inner ears are contained in the *tympano-periotic* bone—shell earbone—actually two bones, the *periotic* and the *tympanic bulla.* Land mammals have these parts imbedded in the skull. The earbone of whales is set apart from the skull, and is attached to it by ligaments, nerves, and blood vessels.

Just how the whale's middle ear functions to transmit the vibrations to the inner ear is still a question. Perhaps the whale's ear responds in much the same way that the ear of terrestrial animals does. Do the vibrations act on the eardrum as they do in humans, reaching the inner ear by means of the amplifying ossicles? The water vibrations are translated for the whale into vibrations of the solid external meatus, which are transmitted by the tympanic membrane to the ossicles.

The middle ear is modified in still another way. It is partly surrounded by cavities filled with a "foam" resembling beaten egg white. These spaces communicate with the middle ear cavity, so that the pressure in both is equal. The loose bony attachment together with the foam is thought to prevent the transmission of sound waves from the skull to the earbone.

The tympano-periotic bone also contains the *cochlea* (the snail-shaped sense organ for hearing) and the semicircular canals, which are necessary for equilibrium. The cochlea contains both the sensory cells and the auditory nerve, and a branch of this nerve connects with the semicircular canals.

This is very similar to the arrangement in land mammals, but there are some important differences. For example, the sensory cells at the bottom of the cochlea, which are stimulated by the high tones, are especially large, and each of them receives its own nerve fiber, whereas in humans one nerve fiber supplies many cells. These same sensory elements are also well developed in other animals sensitive to high-pitched tones: bats, mice, and cats. The auditory nerves that carry impulses to the hearing center in the brain are especially large—the largest of any nerves of odontocetes—and the nerve-fibers, of wide diameter, are built for an unusually rapid transmission of nerve impulses. When we study the structures in the brain—the hearing center in the cortex, sub-centers, and nerve tracts—we find that they are exceptionally large.

About this greater development of cetacean nerve structures involved in hearing, Dr. Tilly Edinger of the Museum of Comparative Zoology at Harvard had this to say: "Of all the groups which during the history of mammals abandoned the normal, terrestrial way of life, bats and whales were the first [to do so]. . . . A unique feature of the cetacean brain is its acoustic system. Only in bats and cetaceans, but most strikingly in the latter, are the acoustic midbrain *colliculi* [the hearing sub-centers] larger than the optic pair." (In man the sub-centers for hearing and sight are of equal size.)

Further, and according to Dr. Winthrop Kellogg, Professor of Experimental Psychology at Florida State University, the hearing sense-organ of the bottlenose dolphin "has undergone a remarkable adaptation in the course of geologic time," and its "marvellously sensitive organ" is especially equipped to receive vibrations in water.

William E. Schevill and his wife, Dr. Barbara Lawrence of the Woods Hole Oceanographic Institute, decided to give dolphins a hearing test. In the laboratories of Marineland, Florida, they trained dolphins to come up for food (a fish) on a single sound signal, produced by a specially designed instrument. The experimenters gradually increased the pitch of the sound (to limits they couldn't hear) and found that the dolphins responded

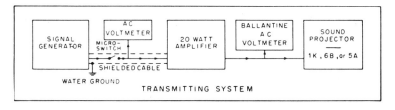

TRANSMITTING SYSTEM

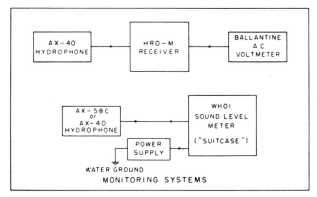

MONITORING SYSTEMS

Apparatus used to test the hearing of a dolphin (*Tursiops truncatus*)

Hearing range of *Tursiops truncatus:* at 120 kilocycles per second, the responses were 100 per cent. After that they fell off rapidly. At 156 kilocycles, the dolphins responded about once in four times

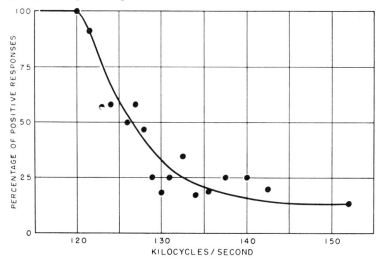

to frequencies (pitches) of 120 kilocycles—120,000 vibrations per second. At frequencies higher than this—up to 156 kilocycles —response began to decrease.

Their tests showed that the range of hearing of whales is perhaps equal to that of bats. Monkeys hear sounds up to frequencies of 33 kilocycles, cats up to 50, mice up to 90, and bats as high as 175 kilocycles. The upper limit of human hearing is about 14 to 16 kilocycles, the sound of a shrill whistle. However, other investigators have found these limits to be somewhat lower, especially for dolphins, as we will see in the next chapter. But the order of relative sensitivity seems to be roughly the same, no matter how hearing is tested.

Using their new technique, Schevill and Lawrence showed that dolphins can pick up sounds below the surface, and can locate the sources of the sounds with great accuracy. They do this by means of two special mechanisms. One, described earlier, is the way the earbone is loosely attached by ligaments to the skull. Unique in whales, this absence of a firm joint partly accounts for their ability to discriminate sound direction, because it serves to isolate one ear from the other. Second, and perhaps even more important, is the albuminous "foam" in the cavities of the middle ear which also enables the whale to perceive the source and direction of sound, a phenomenon called acoustic isolation.

In an experiment to measure the dolphin's directional hearing, two sources of sound were gradually brought closer to each other. When the dolphin went for one, he was rewarded with a fish; when he swam to the other he got nothing. It was found that he was able to distinguish the signals when they were separated by twice the distance possible for humans in air. However, sound travels about five times as fast in water as in air, and the distance between the porpoise's eardrums is half the distance between the eardrum of man, so the experimenters concluded that the dolphin's directional hearing was probably about the same as ours.

Thus it seems that cetaceans' vision is not as highly developed as their hearing, which is acute, and undoubtedly plays a most important role in their staying alive, for they depend largely on their hearing for feeding, direction-finding, depth perception, and communication with one another.

Smell is the most important sense of fish; it is relatively unimportant for whales. It is not a matter of life and death, just as it is not for man and other primates. To be sure, it helps us enjoy our food and some of the finer things of life such as the scent of flowers, new-mown hay, or burning logs. But smell is not essential to life, and people who have lost this sense are deprived of only one of life's special pleasures.

Man's organ of smell is located in the upper part of the nasal cavity, which contains specialized nerve cells that are stimulated by odorous particles in the air. To distinguish a faint odor we sniff the air up into this olfactory (smell) chamber so that the particles can reach the sense organ. Compared with other sense organs, both the olfactory organ and its center in the brain are small. In this regard, Dr. Edinger comments: "Cetaceans are also comparable, physiologically, to the higher primates in that their olfactory organ [and its representation in the brain cortex] are reduced . . ."

And Dr. Slijper has this to say: "We need not waste much time on the sense of smell which is completely lacking in Odontocetes and rudimentary in Mysticetes." Since whales have no organ in the blowhole comparable to our nasal sense organ, it is possible they sense smell through the tongue, and that it is more like taste than smell. Fishes, which have a highly developed sense of smell, can detect the odor of particles dissolved in water, so that their sense organs for smell must also function similarly to the taste buds on our tongues.

During the evolutionary development of land animals from sea animals, the senses of taste and smell, probably combined during life in the water, became separated, and smell came to be perceived through odorous particles diffused in the air. When re-entrants went back to the water, their olfactory organs may have become useless and finally disappeared. This is suggested by the fact that rudimentary organs of smell are still present in baleen whales, and in sea cows these organs are well developed. Also, baleen whales have small outpouchings in the blowhole cavity that are covered with olfactory *epithelium,* and one of the skull bones, the *ethmoid* (found in man in the roof of the nose)—a sieve-like plate for the passage of olfactory nerves—is still present. But in toothed whales there are no remnants of this organ. These whales depend more on their hearing and vision for food-finding.

At the base of the tongue in cetaceans there are elevated structures called *papillae.* These contain taste buds, the same as in man and herbivorous animals. The sense of taste has not been studied in whales, chiefly because carnivorous animals that gulp their food usually have a poor sense of taste. So any selection of food the whale makes is done before it has a chance to taste it. This might explain the strange inedibles sometimes found in ceta-cean stomachs: feathers, pieces of wood, paper, fruit stones, and even a bouquet of flowers have been found in the stomachs of common dolphins from the Black Sea. Even in captivity, such odd objects as a yo-yo and a plastic beach tube were swallowed by a pilot whale. From the small size of the nerve at the back of the tongue, it is again inferred that whatever tasting a whale may do, the sensation must be of minor importance.

Even less is known about the skin—a multiple sense organ through which we experience pain, cold, and heat as well as touch. We take it for granted that whales must experience these sensations. From observations of the behavior of dolphins and pilot whales in captivity, it is thought that they must have a very good sense of touch. They seem to enjoy being stroked by their attendants and trainers. In fact, Dr. Lilly found that bodily con-tact between the keeper and the animal is one sure way of making friends with it, and a requirement for training it. In addition, they stroke each other in their love play, using their flippers and

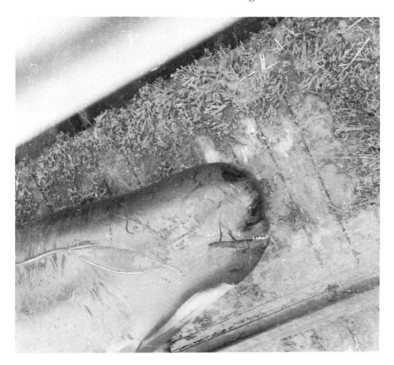

"Melon" and eye slits of North Atlantic Pilot whale

snouts. Like other animals, they also rub themselves against rough surfaces such as planks, stones, and tortoises' shells. The two beluga whales in the New York Aquarium are provided with large boulders on which they are often seen to rub themselves. We inquired about the scratches on their skins and were told that these were the result of this rubbing activity. And in Marine-land, Florida, street-cleaning brushes are fixed to the tank bottom for use as "scratching posts." Like small children, they delight in being hosed, and like many other animals, including your pet cat, they like to be rubbed with a brush.

Certain parts of the whale's body are especially sensitive. One, called the "melon," is a fatty cushion above the snout (found only in toothed whales) that is well supplied with nerves and is assumed to be very sensitive to touch. In baleen whales the few bristles in the upper jaws may function as "feelers." Rorquals also have small bumps on the tip of the snout and on the upper and lower lips, and these bumps contain sensory cells of a kind that would indicate special touch sensitivity. Because the flukes have large and conspicuous nerves, it is assumed that this is another sensitive area for detecting variations in water pressure.

Dr. Lilly also suggests that the dolphin's ability to maintain laminar flow or low resistance by adjusting its flexible skin must depend upon special "touch" nerve endings. This would mean that in the event of beginning turbulence, these nerve endings would be stimulated, and by local reflex action the muscle layer inside the blubber would react so as to shift the blubber and overlying skin, thereby reducing the turbulence. This would complement the damping action Kramer reported to be inherent in the structure of the skin itself.

10

Whistles, Clicks, Echoes

THE FACT THAT DOLPHINS produce sounds is not a modern discovery. Ages ago, Aristotle knew that a dolphin, when taken out of the water, "gives a squeak and moans in the air . . . [and] this creature has a voice, for it is furnished with a lung and a windpipe." Yet he clearly stated what he meant by "voice," adding: "but its tongue is not loose, nor has it lips, so as to give utterance to an articulate sound." Pliny the Elder also agreed that for a voice "they have a moan like a human being."

The "rediscovery" in modern times that porpoises and dolphins have "voices" came during World War II when the United States Navy, in order that its ships could be forewarned about approaching enemy submarines, found a way to detect underwater sounds with a hydrophone, an underwater microphone. By means of this listening instrument, sound waves could be picked up at great distances in deep water. Called SOFAR, a contraction for *So*und *Fi*xing *A*nd *R*anging, it made possible the rapid reception over many miles of otherwise inaudible sounds.

Frequently enough to be disturbing, however, sounds were reported whose origin could not be identified by patrol vessels, and sometimes the sounds would mysteriously disappear shortly after they were heard and before any investigation could be made. It was then that someone thought that the clicking and creaking noises might be due to dolphins and not at all to ships' propellers. Since, as we know, porpoises travel in schools, or pods, by the thousand, their collective sounds could well have been mistaken for exploding missiles or the engines of enemy submarines.

Once investigations into these sounds were undertaken it became clear that the sea was far from silent, and that a variety of creatures—many fish and crustaceans especially—produced noises. These were not just grunts, moans, and squeaks but they resembled, according to Dr. Slijper, "falling stones, ships' hooters, rattling chains" and grating saws. There was as yet no inkling as to the biological meaning of these noises.

The first hint that porpoises might have a built-in system of navigating by means of echoes of their own sounds came in 1947 when Arthur F. McBride, then curator of Marine Studios in St. Augustine, Florida, noted that the bottlenose dolphin would avoid a net with a fine mesh, but not one with a ten-inch mesh. It occurred to him that these animals, like bats, depended on echolocation when visibility was poor. (That bats found their way in absolute darkness by listening to the echoes of their own sounds was first recorded by the Italian scientist, Lazzaro Spallanzani, in the eighteenth century.)

If you have never heard the echo of your own voice, the next time you are in an enclosed space such as a tunnel, a cave, or a valley surrounded by steep hills or mountains, shout your name and the sound will bounce back to your ears. You can do this just for fun, but you do not depend on echoes to avoid obstacles because you have good eyes to help you get about safely. A blind person taps his cane on the pavement to help him locate and avoid, by the sound, objects that might be in his way, but this is a crude and not very dependable way of navigation.

Even if their eyes were better than they are, great whales and porpoises would still find themselves in impenetrable darkness during deep dives. And while swimming in muddy waters, which they themselves stir up, their eyes would be all but useless for locating fish, for judging distances, or for avoiding collisions with submerged obstacles. Imagine a collision of a massive fin whale with a huge rock, an iceberg, or a ship bottom! Also, dolphins entering harbors, bays, or shallow river estuaries encounter many hazards in the form of anchored and moving ships, buoys, docks, piers, and pilings, which we know they readily avoid. And the sperm whale does not crash into the floor of the sea at the great depths to which it is known to dive for food.

Studies of the bottlenose dolphin in several laboratories—notably at the Marine Laboratories of Florida State University—have shown that these animals do produce sounds which they use for echo ranging. The first thing that had to be established was whether porpoises could hear sounds in the high ranges required for echolocation in water. These supersonic or ultrasonic sounds are due to vibrations of extremely high frequency that are mostly beyond our hearing range. It must be remembered that the myriad sounds produced by other animals, the sound of waves, of ships' propellers, and of the rush of water against the body of a rapidly swimming porpoise, would mask or confuse all but the highest "tones."

In 1947, Dr. F. C. Fraser, of the British Museum of Natural History, reported that since a school of porpoises invariably sped off at the sound produced by a supersonic depth finder, their ears could pick up these high frequency sounds. Then in the early 1950's Schevill and Lawrence tested the hearing of dolphins which, you remember, they trained to come for food at a signal. From their own tests of the upper hearing limit of the porpoise, Winthrop N. Kellogg and Robert Kohler of Florida State University concluded in 1952: "The porpoise may resemble the bat, although within a somewhat lower range, since the bat can probably hear sounds up to 120,000" cycles per second.

Finding the idea intriguing that whales and porpoises could use SONAR (a contraction of the words *So*und *Na*vigation and *R*anging) as a part of life, Dr. Kellogg, Florida State University's Professor of Experimental Psychology, went on to echo-ranging experiments. In his book, *Porpoises and Sonar,* he wrote: "If true, it means that human beings did not invent navigation by sound in the ocean. The cetaceans probably evolved it and were using it for millions of years before the idea ever dawned upon man."

Before going on to the porpoise's echo-ranging, let us consider how man locates echoes beneath the surface of the ocean. SONAR is a method of navigation by submarines; it is also used in depth-sounding and, commercially, as a means of locating schools of fish. It works somewhat this way: a train of signals or pings is repeated in quick succession from an underwater transducer, an instrument that transmits vibrations in water. These pings are usually ultrasonic, and their echoes are reflected back to the source from a submerged object or target. The "target" could be any solid object such as a ship, an underwater mine, an

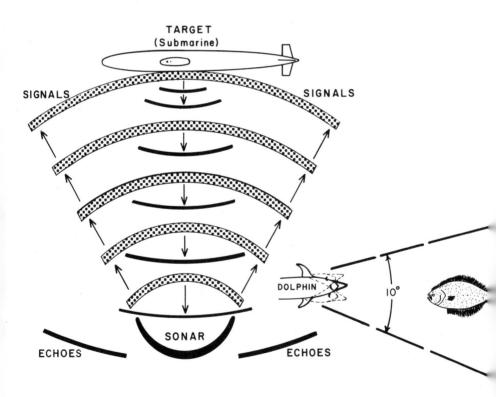

iceberg, the bottom of the ocean, or a school of fish. The echoes are then translated by electronic equipment and are "read" from an oscillograph as electrical pulses on a screen; they may be reproduced with a magnetic tape recorder and played back; or the electronic waves may be photographed for permanent recording. From such readings, the distance, and to some extent the shape, of the echoing target may be determined.

SONAR works on the same principle as RADAR (*R*adio *D*irection *A*nd *R*anging) except that in the latter the emitting and receiving signals are short radio waves, while in the former they are ultrasonic vibrations since RADAR does not work in water. SONAR also differs from SOFAR, which is limited to underwater listening without the emission of echo-ranging signals.

Some sounds the porpoise produces can be heard in air, but others have been heard only since the development of the hydrophone. The noises picked up are amplified and passed through electronic filters which screen out the lower frequencies. The remaining higher frequencies are fed into an ultrasonic analyzer and the sound is broken down into its component parts according to tone (high or low pitch) and intensity (loudness or softness). By means of an instrument called a cathode-ray oscilloscope, the sounds can be "seen" on a screen as vertical streaks or "pips" of varying heights, indicating their intensity. The pips also are ranged on a horizontal scale showing the frequencies in kilocycles per second. As the pips streak across the screen they are photographed, and a "picture" of the sound "spectrum" is produced.

At the same time, the audible components (lower screened-out frequencies) are heard through a loud speaker, while the ultrasonic (inaudible) sounds are recorded on magnetic tape. When the tape is played back at lower speeds—one-fourth, one-eighth, and down to one-sixty-fourth—the sounds become audible. For example, if the true frequency is 80,000 cycles per second and the speed at which it is reproduced is one-sixteenth

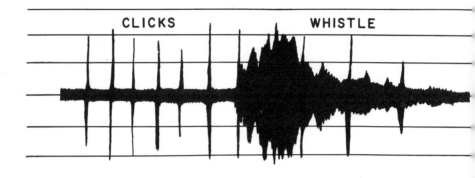

4800 CYCLES PER SECOND

Porpoise sounds (clicks and whistles) as they appear on an
oscillographic screen, translated electronically

the original, it is changed to a frequency of 5,000 cycles per second; at the same time the sound lasts 16 times as long as at the higher frequency, making it audible to most persons.

Also the oscilloscope picture can be expanded by reducing the speed at which the film is run. The sound and the picture are compared during later study.

By such methods, requiring the instruments and talents of electronic and acoustical engineers, porpoise noises have been broken down into two main kinds: whistles and clicks.

Listened to on records and tape, the sounds of captive porpoises have been described, depending on the listener, as: mewing, rasping, barking, crackling, clicking, clacking, and yelping; or as grunts, chirps, snorts, blats, squeaks, squawks; some hear them as "sputtering," "woodpecking," and "creaking-door" and "rusty-hinge" sounds. Then some hear "humanoid" or "mimics of human laughter" while others say they "merely sound like a lot of radio static." (In addition, there is the jaw clap—the sound produced by Flipper, the television star—which can be seen as well as heard.)

These descriptions show how people hear dolphin sounds, but have little to do with their analysis as whistles and clicks by the physicist, and they do not help us to grasp their meaning. It is like trying to understand a strange language by asking different persons to imitate the sound of the words.

By the detailed analysis already described, the whistle has been found to last about half a second, and to have one or more of several pitch patterns. The "melody" heard most often from Dr. Kellogg's porpoises, which he says resembles the "cheep of a canary," ranges over an octave, roughly between 7,000 and 15,000 cycles per second. In other words, some of the whistle is audible to the human ear, but much of it is believed to be in the ultrasonic range. And because of its continuously changing pitch, the whistle must produce a continuously changing echo; it is, therefore, described in the language of the physicist as a frequency-modulated SONAR.

The clicks, by far the most common of underwater sounds, and described as the "rusty-hinge" or "creaking-door" noise, have been identified by so many people that these terms are now used in technical reports. The bottlenose dolphin produces this sound as a series of rapid clicks or pings, the individual clicks varying in number from five to several hundred per second. At the higher rates they may be heard more as a groan or a bark. While part of it is in the sonic range, physical analysis shows that the major component of the sound is in the high-frequency ultrasonic range—up to 120 kilocycles, with occasional vibrations reaching 200 kilocycles. Because these sounds are given off in bursts, or groups, they are called the pulse-modulated echo-ranging signals contrasted with the frequency-modulated whistle. (Compare the picture of a series of such clicks and their echoes on page 194, with that of the whistle, composed of different frequencies or pitches, on page 192.)

The rapid succession of short pings, with time allowed for each pulse to reflect back its own echo, is the ideal method for echo ranging. The porpoise does use the frequency-modulated

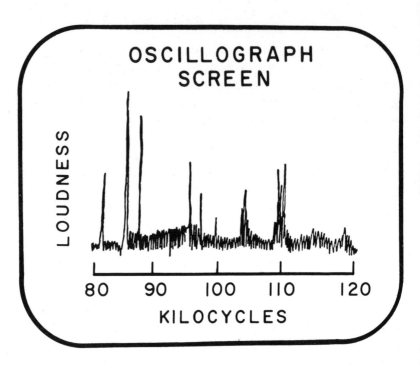

OSCILLOGRAPH
SCREEN

LOUDNESS

80   90   100   110   120
KILOCYCLES

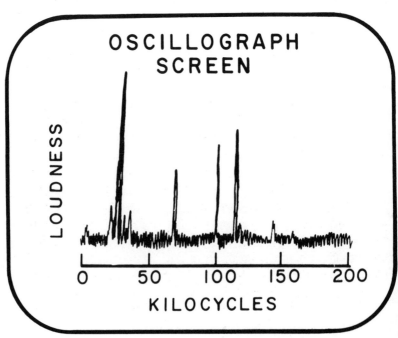

OSCILLOGRAPH
SCREEN

LOUDNESS

0   50   100   150   200
KILOCYCLES

(whistle) method but, as we have seen, these sounds are ineffective against the innumerable background noises of the sea. That's why basketball and football referees and swimming pool lifeguards use a high-pitched shrill whistle. In all the noise, even their loudest shouts would not attract attention.

Also, the higher the frequency the shorter the wave length, and therefore the shorter each echo. The advantage is greater accuracy in identifying the size and shape of the target. On the other hand, waves of lower frequency travel greater distances, and if interfering noises are absent, they are more useful in detecting distant objects and so more suitable for long-range direction finding.

Thus the porpoise has the advantage of a double system of echolocation: one for close range and detailed examination of an object, the other for general orientation at sea.

Not only bottlenoses but other dolphins and larger whales have been heard to make noises: at a Symposium in 1963 held at Bimini, Bahama Islands, Dr. Kenneth S. Norris of the University of California listed—in addition to two species of Tursiops—the common dolphin, Baird's dolphin, the long-snouted dolphin, the spotted dolphin, the Pacific striped dolphin, and the pilot whale, the beluga, and the killer. Sounds have also been ascribed to the sperm whale, the largest of the toothed whales. And while Dr. Norris stated that no echo-locating sounds have definitely been reported for baleen whales, Dr. Kellogg mentions that "flute tone" sounds have been heard from fin whales, but only during the mating season; they may not be used for echolocation at all.

Descriptions of the noises made by whales in their natural environment are even more colorful than those of the dolphin in captivity, perhaps because they are more casually, less critically, and so less accurately observed. To different observers, the squeaks of the common dolphin sounded like "playing mice," the beluga whale's sounds were like "musical glasses badly played," and the noises made by the pilot whale ranged from a "loud smacking noise" to "the peevish whining of a young child."

In 1957, a lucky encounter with five sperm whales enabled two scientists from the Woods Hole Oceanographic Institution in Massachusetts to listen to their sounds from the vessel *Atlantis,* off the North Carolina coast. Before the whales were sighted, muffled smashing noises were heard, about half a second apart, and were at first thought to be a hammering somewhere on board. But soon the whales appeared, and Worthington and Schevill (with the ship's engines turned off) hooked up the echo-ranging receiver. The smashing noise was then followed by a second grating sound of low pitch "which reminded some of a rusty hinge creaking," lasting as much as five seconds.

Schevill and his collaborators from Woods Hole also have recorded sounds of fin whales, humpbacks, and Atlantic right whales and have found them to be extremely low.

The echo-ranging patterns in different species must represent adaptations to particular needs. For example, the lower sonic frequencies may be more useful to the deep-diving sperm whale feeding on the giant squid, while the higher frequencies better serve the purposes of the dolphin in selecting its food close to the surface.

Early in his work with dolphins, Dr. Kellogg realized that neither cement aquarium tanks nor chance observations of the animals at sea were ideal conditions for the study of echolocation: interfering echoes bounced off from the tank walls, and conditions at sea could not be adequately controlled. By persuading the proper authorities, he obtained funds to construct a large outdoor pool, or enclosure, at the Marine Laboratories of Florida State University, some forty miles south of Tallahassee at Alligator Harbor on the Gulf of Mexico. The black coastal mud that formed the sides and bottom of the pool was soft, sound-absorbent, and so reflected a minimum of its own echoes. In this echo-free "porpoise laboratory" Dr. Kellogg could observe the same porpoises for long periods of time in an environment as close to their natural one as could be achieved artificially. All of the necessary listening and recording equipment was set up for controlled long-range experiments. The possibility that the animals would use their vision during the tests was eliminated by the turbidity of the shoal water in the harbor, cloudy and brownish from the spring through the fall months.

In this setting the experimenters studied the porpoises' sonar responses to a variety of immersed objects, and the pings that the animals beamed on these objects were recorded. In general, they found that the sonar sounds differed from man-made sonar in three ways: the rate per second of the individual pings, the modulation of their intensity, and their frequency components.

The targets used to test echo-ranging were hanging vertical poles, buckshot, streamlined wooden shapes that could be lowered into the water without a splash, clear plastic sheets, food fish (mullet), and a human swimmer. To determine the effect of surface splashing without insertion of a target, measured quantities of water were dropped into the pool (as little as a half-spoonful caused a single train of signals, while a stream from a half-inch hose caused continuous "alarm" whistling).

A porpoise swimming in this very muddy water, either in daytime or on an overcast night, could distinguish between glass-covered and open passageways in a barrier, could navigate successfully through the vertical poles in its path, but would approach food and a human swimmer. When the buckshot was dropped, high-frequency signals followed the splash, but in the absence of food the animal paid no more attention to it. It seemed that, realizing that the disturbance represented neither food nor danger, it turned off its sonar.

One of the most interesting of these experiments was conducted with Albert, an adolescent bottlenose about 7 feet long and weighing about 300 pounds. Together with Betty, an older companion, Albert was kept in the enclosure for over a year. Early in their captivity, for some reason they rejected the usual mullet and were given instead another salt-water fish called spot, abundant in Chesapeake Bay. Taking advantage of this preference for the 6-inch spot over the 12-inch mullet, Dr. Kellogg set up his experiment.

He mounted a plywood screen at the end of the dock so that about two inches of its lower end dipped into the water. From behind this the fishes could be submerged by hand, without being seen by the porpoise. The position of the two kinds of target fishes was alternated at random, presenting the porpoise with a size-discrimination problem that tested his ability to choose between the positive stimulus (the spot) and the negative stimulus (the mullet).

Albert came to each experimental session not having eaten for 24 hours. Behind the screen were two experimenters: E-1 and E-2. E-1 lay face down on the dock; his job was to present the target. E-2, stopwatch in hand, supervised the recording equipment. A trial began when Albert was completely "ready," meaning that he came to the top of the water, either lying on the surface, waiting, or "treading water." At that moment E-1 immersed the fish, giving the signal "In" to E-2. When Albert touched the fish, E-1 said "contact" and as soon as Albert took the fish came the third signal, "Take." All this was done to time Albert's response as well as to record his choice of fish.

The sounds, picked up by the underwater listening gear and translated electronically, showed that Albert sent out bursts of signals before lunging toward the screen. During each session, Albert was offered the two fish from 14 to 27 times—the number of trials depending upon Albert's appetite at the particular session.

After 14 sessions and a total of 271 trials, the chart showed that in the first 7 sessions Albert made a few errors, but these decreased (showing learning with each session) until in the last 7 sessions he invariably selected the spot fish rather than the mullet. In 140 trials he didn't make a single incorrect choice.

At the end of this experiment, Albert was tested in two

sessions when the two fishes were presented so that the mullet protruded only 6 inches—the same length as the spot. Albert immediately began making errors: his ability to discriminate was disrupted.

Dr. Kellogg concluded that Albert had made his selection on the basis of the fish size, and that the choice was made by echo-ranging and not by another sense. The evidence for this was pretty conclusive: the recordings showed differences in the pings; Albert's scoring was the same during day and night sessions; smell was not involved because the stimuli remained the same throughout the experiment; Albert was sometimes seen to turn his head to the right and left while approaching the fish, as if in an effort to compare the echoes.

The nature of the whistles and clicks is being investigated, and is as yet poorly understood, but scientists agree that the porpoise has a highly refined sonar system, far more accurate and varied than anything yet made by man. However, much remains unexplained about how and where the sounds are produced. Any explanation has to take into account that cetaceans have no vocal cords, so their sounds must be produced by some other mechanism in the larynx or the nasal passages, including the blowhole. And the anatomy of these parts is extremely intricate.

Furthermore, certain observations add to the difficulties of explaining what happens during sound production: 1) certain sounds—"creaks"—are heard whether the blowhole is open or closed; 2) the frequencies (tones) of these creaks are different when the blowhole is open and when it is closed; 3) the truly high frequency echo-location bursts seem to be produced only with the blowhole closed; 4) in at least one animal, the click seemed to be produced on one side and the whistle on the other, simultaneously, although further evidence of this is needed. All these occurrences show that porpoises must have more than one vibrating structure, and that the powerful blowhole valve is only one of these.

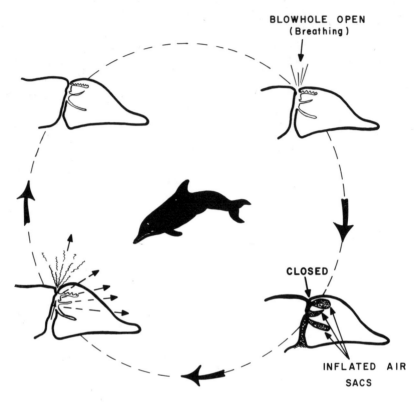

BLOWHOLE OPEN
(Breathing)

CLOSED

INFLATED AIR
SACS

Position of blowhole and air sacs during breathing and whistling

When trained dolphins "sing out" on command—standing on their flukes and giving out with what has been called a Bronx cheer—the vibrating mechanism is the blowhole lips, just as your lips vibrate when you blow air through them from your lungs. This is what probably happens when the sounds are produced in air, with the blowhole partly open, but when the animal is under water, where it is most of the time, the blowhole is always closed. So if underwater sounds are caused by the passage of air, then it should be possible to see a stream of bubbles during the noise-making. Some observers claim to have seen such streams of bubbles, but Dr. Kellogg found none while picking up the sounds with a hydrophone, and he points out further that even when the sounds are made in air, it does not mean that they are initiated by or at the blowhole, any more than a singer's lips produce the notes that pass through them—the sound being produced by the vibration of the vocal cords in the larynx.

Regardless of details, most scientists agree that whales produce their echo-location clicks by manipulating air under pressure. The structure of the nasal passages lends itself to this idea. Below the blowhole valve there are air pockets which extend to the side of the opening toward the snout, and there are tongue-like projections into the opening which are controlled by muscles and may be set vibrating. In addition, there is an internal valve, at the lower part of the nasal passage, which could vibrate in the same way as the outer valve. Under pressure from the thorax, the air must be pushed upward from the lungs through the trachea, and as it goes past the various vibrating structures, sounds are produced. Also, the frequency and intensity of the sounds must be controlled by varying amounts of pressure on the air in the pockets. With the blowhole closed, the air has to recirculate, alternately filling and emptying the air sacs in such a way as to produce sounds of low frequency at low air pressure, and sounds of high frequency under high pressure. When needed, the animal may emit sounds from one side, in order to achieve more precise positioning of the target for getting echoes from that side. It has been seen, for example, that in scanning its environment the porpoise will swing its head rapidly to one side or the other. This may help it to hear, and through hearing, to locate and find (or avoid) food or obstacles.

Concluding his paper (1964) at the Symposium at Bimini, Bahamas (1963), Dr. Norris said: "We now know that some odontocete whales, and probably many of them, are sophisticated, acoustically oriented animals possessed of very refined adaptations relating to this sense."

One other finding indicating that the region below the

blowhole may be the source of sound is the observation by both Dr. Norris and Dr. Lilly that the clicks come out of, or from a place near, the top of the head. Dr. Norris found that when a porpoise was blindfolded by placing suction cups over its eyes, and the target fish was presented below the level of its face or mouth, it had difficulty in locating it. The difficulty disappeared when the fish was placed on a line with the porpoise's mouth or just above it, even though it was blindfolded. This means, according to Dr. Norris, that the clicks must be directed toward the target somewhere from the forehead or melon, and Dr. Kellogg says: "Even assuming the sounds are not highly directional, a target which is screened from the source of the sounds by the animal's own body would furnish poor or garbled echoes."

Different species are capable of producing different sounds; this is apparently related to subtle differences in the vibrating structures. For instance, in the common (harbor) porpoise the air sacs are thick-walled with deep folds, while in the killer they are much thinner and less folded. This might be compared to voice differences determined in individual humans by the length and thickness of the vocal cords, the size of the voice box, and the resonance spaces in the head.

In addition to producing sounds for echolocation, the bottlenose dolphin makes sounds (some audible to humans) in order to communicate. After analyzing and studying these in great detail, Dr. Lilly has divided them into three classes, according to the conditions under which the animal emits them: some are sent out spontaneously when the animal is alone; others on hearing the sounds of another animal nearby; and still others in response to something the observer is doing.

Both whistles and clicks, but rarely quacks or blats, are heard when the animal is in isolation. Since these range in frequency between 4,000 and 18,000 cycles per second, some are within the range of human hearing. In exchanges with another dolphin, the emissions are frequent and complete, the two ani-

mals alternating as in "conversation," with simultaneous emissions ("duets") being rare. When such whistles are played back
at one-eighth the original speed, they "sound something like an
air-raid or police siren whose tone shifts or warbles."

The whistles, of which there are many kinds, are often distress signals such as from a baby porpoise separated from its
mother; when these are heard, the companions of the distressed
animal immediately search for the source, which may also be a
shark, an injury, or an inability to surface. If it is a shark, they
will attack it and drive it off or kill it; or they will push the injured
one to the surface while carrying on whistle exchanges with it.

Sounds of the third class—squawks, quacks, and blats—
occur usually during "emotional situations such as in courtship
and violent play," or when pleasurable sensations are produced
experimentally by stimulating the brain electrically—experiments
by Dr. Lilly, to be described in the next chapter. It seems that
these sounds are expressions of intense pleasure, or possibly anger.
In either case, they are in response to an "intense emotional situation." Also, it has been noted that these sounds may occur at
the same time as whistles. Dr. Lilly interprets these findings as
evidence that the dolphin has at least two separately controlled
sonic (audible) emitters: one for the production of clicks and
one for whistles—both for purposes of communication. The animal produces these sounds with the blowhole open, in air, and
they are accompanied by small bubbles; and, he concludes:
"That the dolphin has precise and accurate control of these
emissions is no longer in doubt."

11

Of Brains and "Talking" Dolphins

IN THE QUARTER of a century that the captive bottlenose dolphin has been closely studied by scientists, its "box-office rating" as a performer has far outreached that of the seal, elephant, and ape: as a lovable creature it has captured the hearts of millions.

Those who have worked with, trained, cared for, and "lived with" dolphins have marvelled at what may now be called the "dolphin personality." Its captive cousins, the pilot whales, have shared both the glory and the adjectives used to describe them: friendly, delightful, genial, gay, jolly, pleasant, gentle, kindly, amiable, inquisitive, inventive, playful, frolicsome, humorous, prankish, and "intelligent." These are qualities we generally attribute to people, and indeed dolphins have been called "people of the sea."

The bottlenose dolphin has a reputation for being a great mimic and for displaying a highly developed sense of humor; some say that the dolphin is actually laughing at us. Take the incident filmed and recently presented by Dr. Lilly to an audience of doctors meeting in Florida, in which the "joke" was apparently on himself. As is Dr. Lilly's habit in studying his dolphins, one day he jumped into the specially constructed saltwater enclosure where one was swimming about unconcernedly. But on seeing that Dr. Lilly was doing the dog-paddle, the dolphin veered around to face him and began clapping his flippers in "pat-a-cake" fashion, as if burlesquing the movements of a human swimming. What was remarkable about the scene, Dr. Lilly emphasized, was that this rakish mimicry was spontaneous:

the dolphin had not been trained for this amusing performance, and had never before displayed it. (Some workers would be skeptical about such an interpretation, since this motion is characteristically a courtship gesture, and does not have to be learned.)

Many stories are told of dolphins teasing another tank occupant, or human, whether a spectator or familiar attendant. One young porpoise in Florida's Marineland was seen tugging a five-foot shark by its tail, only to drop the shocked beast in the middle of the tank. Another lifted a large turtle off the bottom with its snout and stood it up, rolled it across the pool to the opposite wall, and then repeated the stunt. In the oceanarium at Marineland of the Pacific, bottlenoses, when they are not hungry, will throw fish back at their feeders. And when new exhibit fish are introduced into the tank, some are captured and eaten, but others are thrown out of the tank alive and unharmed. It is said that one of these was "deliberately" saved for bouncing off the head of the aquarium director!

Dolphins are reputed not to like persons dressed in black (some say their "favorite" color is blue) and an occasional oceanarium visitor in black garb may be treated to a shower of water and pebbles, squirted at him by a willful porpoise.

Then there is the case of the dolphin whose echo-locating ability was being studied while she was blindfolded. The procedure was to signal her to approach the side of the pool to have suction cups placed on her eyes. She would come when called, but each day would stop just a little farther away from the appointed spot, forcing the experimenter to lean over more and more to reach her, until finally one day he came near to falling in. Such teasing actions are common, and trainers will sometimes find themselves drenched by a dolphin's dive, apparently purposefully to splash them with water.

Dolphins will also playfully butt or nudge a pelican and pull out a feather to play with. But they do not limit their teasing to the small and helpless. They have been seen to "play with"

Dolphin retrieving rubber ring tossed into the air

moray eels, about four feet long and capable of inflicting serious bites. These eels live in crevices of the rock decorations in the tank, and Mr. Brown and Dr. Norris tell us that the dolphins learn to pull them from their hiding places into the middle of the tank. "There they let the eels slither through their jaws. Once one of the eels turned around and bit the dolphin, who immediately released it, but was back in a few moments playing with the eel again."

Their playfulness does not always have a malicious intent, any more than a kitten's unraveling of knitting while playing with the ball of yarn is an act of mischief. More often they seem to engage in play just for "good clean fun," sometimes chasing each other, engaging in mock fighting, or tossing dead fish or rubber objects into the air and retrieving them the way a dog retrieves a stick. But dolphin play is different in many ways from that of cats and dogs: it is sustained for an hour or more, it is inventive, it is varied for the occasion, it is not done for the sake of reward alone, and it often involves the cooperation of several individuals. Here are a few of the recorded instances of their inventive and social play.

Frankie, Floyd, Mabel, and Myrtle were bottlenose dolphins who often played together. Frankie was playing with a pelican feather which he would release near the bottom of the tank, above the incoming jet of water. As the feather drifted up, it was caught and swept along in the current. Frankie would retrieve the feather and repeat the game over and over, with all the dolphins participating. Sometimes one of them would throw the feather up in the air and catch it as it fell back.

They would also vary this feather play by trying to throw it at spectators behind the rail. Once, when the wet feather stuck to the wall, one of them swam to the side of the pool, jumped out of the water, and maneuvered the feather with the side of his head so that it fell into the water. Then they tried again and again to throw it out, sometimes successfully.

A few days later, Frankie invented a new game: "He swam to the bottom, picked up a pebble 1½″ in diameter, and threw it at one of the customers standing at the edge of the tank. The man threw the pebble back into the pool. Frankie retrieved the pebble and, even though many people were leaning on the railing, he threw it back to the same man. The two went through this routine eight times."

On another occasion, all four were swimming after a three-pound kelp bass when it hid in a crevice. They proceeded to harass it from each end, one porpoise snapping at one end and, as the fish moved, the others snapping at the other end. Finally the bass escaped, racing across the tank with the four porpoises on its tail. While there were many other and more accessible fish, they pursued only this one, except once when they were fooled by a bass of the same size, but they quickly left it and returned to the first victim.

Once Frankie and Floyd were trying to pull a moray eel out from its crevice, working from each side without success. One of the other dolphins left the group, killed a scorpion fish (which has sharp and poisonous spines), and returned with it in his mouth. The bottlenose poked at the eel with the spiney fish and prodded it out of the crevice. Then the dolphins followed it, caught it, took it to the middle of the tank, and released it when the "game" was over.

People are especially attracted to dolphins because they are so responsive to human attention. Once trained in an aquarium, they enjoy being taken through their tricks during "the show," and react like real stage "hams" to loud and enthusiastic applause from the audience. They are capable of a give-and-take relationship with humans and make lovable pets. Some will accept child and even adult riders and will tow a small rubber boat with delighted passengers. Just as readily they will permit themselves to be pulled backward through the water by their flukes, once they recognize that the tugging is done in fun by a friendly person.

Even in the wild, dolphins always have enjoyed a reputation as man's best friend at sea. Many centuries ago the Greek biographer Plutarch wrote: "Though it has no need at all of any man, yet it is a genial friend to all and has helped many."

The frolicking of dolphins around a ship has never failed to fascinate seafarers. Riding the bow waves may well be part of dolphin play—perhaps a way of getting "a free ride"—but to sailors, as to Plutarch, this is a sign of the friendship of dolphins for man, and a good omen. Sea lore is filled with stories of dolphins guiding ships to safety.

There was perhaps more than a grain of truth in the ancient legends, for there is an authenticated story, in modern times, of a now world-famed dolphin in New Zealand waters—a story reconstructed with great care, by the Australian journalist Antony Alpers, from scores of letters and documents, and from conversations with people who gave first-hand accounts of Pelorus Jack.

For twenty-four years this dolphin acted as pilot for ships plying between Wellington on North Island, and Nelson on South Island, separated by Cook Straits and Pelorus Sound. What better friend can man have than a pilot "on call" to navigate him through treacherous shoals? Pelorus Jack did just that every day of those years between 1888 and 1912, accompanying the vessels on their daily trips back and forth between the two ports. At the sound of the ship's horn or motors, he would appear from underwater and guide the steamboats across the Straits. The faster the ship the better he seemed to like it, perhaps because riding the bow waves was more fun. That his services were really needed in these shallow waters was tragically proven in 1909 when the *Penguin,* the fastest of the ships, was wrecked and all seventy-five passengers lost. Where was Pelorus Jack?

Some months before the shipwreck, the dolphin, hurt and bleeding from an injury by the ship's propeller, veered from the side of the craft and raced off to sea. He never again answered the whistle of the *Penguin.* But for the following three years he continued his regular service to the other ships! In 1912, Pelorus Jack did not answer any vessel's whistle, and where he went and how he died no one knows to this day. Nor was its sex ever known—"Jack" may have been a Jill—and only from descriptions of its estimated length of 12 feet, gray back and almost white underside, lack of the typical dolphin beak and, mainly, the white streaks across its body, was it assumed to be a Risso's dolphin.

Most New Zealanders like to think that Pelorus Jack's actions, for what must have been most of a lifetime, were acts of enduring friendship toward *Homo sapiens,* but could it be that Pelorus Jack merely enjoyed coasting on the waves, especially those churned up by the fastest ships? Or perhaps he gloried in the adoring passengers' and crew's shouts of "He's coming!"

Fishermen are only too familiar with porpoises crowding around their boats, especially if they are fishing for mullet or mackerel, two of the favorite foods of porpoises. But sometimes a single porpoise will return to a well-defined locality—a harbor pier or an anchored fishing vessel—seemingly to make only a friendly call. This habit of showing up with expected regularity has been called home ranging, a way of life for some dolphins and for some of them undoubtedly a lifetime habit. Take Snowball, the only captive albino *Tursiops truncatus* in the world and, until she died, in 1965, the star attraction in the Miami Seaquarium. For at least ten years before this prize was captured in 1962, she was seen from time to time in South Carolina's St. Helena Sound. White as driven snow, she could hardly be missed during her periodic calls, but reports by the shrimp boat fishermen, who used to throw her the unwanted fish picked up in the shrimp traps, were ignored as only rumors until Captain Emil Hanson, skipper of the Seaquarium's collecting boat, saw for himself.

The saga of Snowball, beginning in the fall of 1961 and ending with her capture and that of her gray baby, Sonny Boy, in August of the following year, was full of high adventure. During three separate expeditions over many weeks of disappointing trys and legal battles with Beaufort County authorities, one thing was sure: Snowball was unconcernedly cavorting in the waters of St. Helena Sound, and the fishermen welcomed her, if not for herself, then surely because she warded off sharks. Of course Snowball's visits were rewarded with food, but the fishermen saw a desire for human companionship in these regular appearances.

More remarkable than home ranging around fishing vessels are the instances of dolphins befriending divers and bathers, especially children. Opo, a bottlenose dolphin, is perhaps even more famous than Pelorus Jack. For six months her sensational sojourn in Opononi put this township on the world map. Opononi, located inside Hokianga Harbor on the western side of New Zealand's North Island, several miles north of Auckland, is

Snowball and Sonny Boy

a fishing village. The only facilities it had to offer visitors were a small seaside beach, an old wooden hotel, and a motor camp where, during the Christmas holidays (the southern summer), people pitched their tents close to the beach.

In the fall of 1955 Opononi had an unusual visitor. Earlier that year a dolphin had been seen accompanying the fishing boats. She was befriended by the fishermen, who soon discovered that she liked to have her back scratched—with oars, paddles, mops, brushes, or anything available. Opo was a youngster—probably about a year old—and in retrospect people recalled that, through the local practice of dynamiting for fish, a family of dolphins had come to grief some months before Opo arrived. Perhaps she was the only survivor. Opo was not on the hunt for food, when she came to Hokianga Harbor, for, as a matter of fact, the only times she disappeared during her all-too-brief stay in Opononi were when she swam to deeper waters for her meals. And for six months she came every day, just for the sport of it. As Alpers tells the story, Opo "lived in the sea, as free as any wild animal or bird, and no one could have made it do anything it did not want to do but it came and played, and went away, and came of its own free will again."

Fearless and playful, Opo was attracted by the bathers and worked her charm on both children and adults. One day she struck up a friendship with a thirteen-year-old girl whom she startled by chasing her to shore, then slipped between her legs and took her for a ride. (The girl later explained that she thought the dolphin was attracted by her blue swim-flippers.) But Opo didn't limit her playful attention to one special friend. When someone threw her a beach ball, she knew what to do with it: balancing it on her head, she would roll it down her back and, with a flick of her fluke, send it bouncing along the water for 20 feet or more. Then she would race to catch it with her flippers and repeat the performance. She would race the children in a game of "fetch," but most memorable was the day a group of school children, on a picnic with their teacher, were wading in the shallow water. Opo swam right up to them. The children joined hands, making a ring, and Opo once more rose to the occasion: she entered the ring and began circling and "porpoise dancing" to the rhythm of the children's singing.

If the sleepy town of Opononi had few tourists before, it now attracted them by the thousands, and drew up great plans for future accommodations for those who jammed its streets, blocked traffic, and stretched its meager facilities to the bursting point just to have a look at the lovable dolphin. Some visitors even went into the water fully dressed just for the chance to touch her.

While there are many stories of dolphins becoming attached to a single child—usually a boy—Opo was friendly to all humans, old and young alike. The children named her Gay Golphin, and the town, fearful for her safety, posted signs: "WELCOME TO OPONONI, BUT DON'T TRY TO SHOOT OUR GAY GOLPHIN." And just about the day that a law to protect her was to go into effect, making it a crime to hurt her, Opo suddenly disappeared.

A few days later her body was discovered trapped between rocks in a pool farther out in the harbor, where she went to feed. The bereaved inhabitants speculated on the cause of her death. Could she have been stranded there at low tide? Those knowledgeable in such matters knew that no dolphin endowed with echolocation, and especially Opo who was familiar with the tides, would ever be caught in such a situation. The more likely explanation was that her death was caused by an explosion set off accidentally or intentionally in dynamite fishing. The shock of the blast may have stunned her so that she could not surface, or having recovered when the tide was low, she may not have been able to make her way out of the trap (her skin was badly scraped). Either accident could have caused her suffocation.

Opo was laid to rest with a public funeral and her grave was covered with flowers brought by the children. Soon after, another theory of her death was advanced by Mr. Piwai Toi, a Maori farmer. At the height of Opo's popularity he had written an article about her for the Maori journal, *Te Ao Hou*. Mr. Toi was now sure that Opo had committed suicide for two reasons: she had no playmate of her own kind, and, with her love of children, she must have yearned for a baby of her own.

Even assuming that a dolphin as gay as Opo could possibly have had "suicidal thoughts," you now know that her very youth argued against such a theory. For dolphins become adolescents only after three years of age, and don't usually have babies until they are at least five years old. At the time of her death, Opo was only a year-and-a-half old, and if she had been an orphan at the time she first came to Opononi beach, her coming there could have meant that she was searching for her family. Not finding them, she generously gave of her love and friendship to the welcoming humans, who returned it in kind.

Among the stoutest in their praise of dolphins are persons who have come near drowning and recall being "shoved by something" safely to shore. From the time in antiquity when Arion, the Greek poet and singer, lured the dolphin by his song, then jumped overboard to escape the ship's pirates and was carried to safety, many stories of rescues by dolphins have been told. Here are two of them, modern and apparently true.

In the November 1949 issue of *Natural History Magazine* an account appeared of a woman in Florida who was saved from drowning by a dolphin. She had gone bathing alone on a private beach and, while wading waist deep, she was swept off her feet by a strong undertow. She called for help, but with water in her lungs and terribly frightened, her voice was not loud enough. "I realized that, while only about ten feet from shore, there was no way I could make it, and kept thinking, as I gradually lost consciousness, please God can't someone push me ashore. With that, someone gave me a tremendous shove, and I landed on the beach, face down, too exhaused to turn over." After several minutes she was able to turn around; then she saw a porpoise a short distance from shore and a "large fish" a few feet beyond. The woman's story was corroborated by a man who had come running from the public beach, saying he had seen only the last part—what seemed to be a dead body being shoved ashore by a porpoise as if trying to protect it from what he thought was a shark.

The second event happened in 1960 and involved a Florida woman who had fallen overboard off the east coast of Grand

Bahama Island in the West Indies. The account is given by Dr. Winthrop N. Kellogg from a signed personal interview with the near-victim. In this case, the porpoise guided the panicked woman through waters known to be infested by barracuda and shark until she was carried by the tide into shallow water. While this incident occurred at night and was not witnessed, it is one of many that are reported from time to time all over the world.

Since we know from actual observations that porpoises have a tendency to push all sorts of objects—kegs, wooden planks, water-soaked mattresses—it is not hard to believe that they would also push a drowning person. Perhaps as an instinctive act of preservation of its own kind, as we discussed earlier, a mother dolphin will nudge a newborn infant to the surface if it delays in swimming upward to breathe, and a group have been seen taking turns holding up an injured or handicapped member of the pod. As we saw, this is so persistent an urge that a dead infant will also be pushed for hours by its mother or "aunts." It is just as possible that the shoving of an object through the water is part of their natural playfulness, and "coming to the aid" of a drowning or even a motionless body is no more significant in the life of a porpoise than pushing a mattress. In these terms, we can understand the determination of a group of porpoises that had to be driven off because they insisted on pushing six downed American flyers, drifting on a rubber raft, into certain death on an island occupied by the Japanese during World War II. This story was told by Dr. George Llano in his book, *Airmen Against the Sea*.

Even if in the eyes of humans such "rescues" appear to be "good deeds," "signs of friendship," or "acts of mercy," it is probably a mistake to interpret them as deliberate, intentional, or consciously helpful acts. For even the amazing porpoises, as the editor of *Natural History Magazine* wrote: ". . . do not ordinarily have any acquaintanceship with human beings, do not know whether they breathe air or water, and cannot be supposed to feel love or sympathy for them." We must even consider the possibility that if the playful shoving should be directed out to sea instead of toward the shore, we would never hear of it.

Scientists tell us that all dolphins are not gay and friendly, and those that are, are not always so. The first encounter with a human being may be far from friendly. As often happens with newly caught captives in aquaria, dolphins, like other wild creatures, are shy and wary of man. It is only after days or weeks of human contact and friendly reassurance by the attendants that humans are gradually accepted. Usually the dolphins keep their distance and show their timidity by not accepting offered food. Dr. Kellogg describes the behavior of one young captive:

It made a great to-do about coming after a fish held in the hand but did not have nerve enough to follow through. In fact, it behaved exactly like a little boy trying to make his first dive from a diving board. It would orient toward me, take a good look, and then surge forward with tremendous enthusiasm. But before it got close enough to make a pass at the fish, it would stop completely or else swim by two or three feet away.

After a dozen or so tries it finally came close enough to get the fish.

Some porpoises never fully adjust to life in captivity. A case in point was Betty, Albert's older companion in Dr. Kellogg's pool in Alligator Harbor. While other animals learned to accept confinement in small enclosures, when separation was necessary, Betty reacted badly, developing what in humans would be called neurotic behavior. Typical was "a kind of up-and-down motion without going anywhere," described as the "rocking-horse movement." Her tail thrusts, which would normally have pushed her forward, were apparently counter-balanced by simultaneous backward movements of the flippers. At one time she refused to accept any food, and even in the larger pool would not consistently take a fish from an attendant, sometimes turning away from him and going through the rocking routine. Because of her lack of cooperation they were never able to use her for experiments, and she could be made to "work" only by "punishment" (lack of food) rather than by food reward. "She seemed to be telling us in no uncertain terms that we were no longer her friends."

Even whales that start out jolly and friendly may for some reason begin to throw tantrums and sulk, as did Bimbo, a pilot whale in Marineland of the Pacific, captured in 1959 off Santa Catalina Island. For four years he was a star performer, the largest whale in captivity and a companion of Bubbles, a female. Then suddenly, according to an Associated Press story in February 1965, Bimbo "went haywire" and even stopped eating. In fact, the doctor diagnosed his trouble as a mental disorder with a name describing a similar (manic-depressive) condition in humans. His moods alternated between "complete apathy, to wild, aggressive agitation." Mr. David Brown, Marineland's curator of mammals, attributed the whale's condition to middle age and work fatigue from over-training. Under proper medical care, and given drugs to quiet his nerves and lift his mood, Bimbo was cured, but he will never work again; having earned his retirement, he has been "put out to pasture."

If you have never been captivated by the "dolphin personality," a few stories may suggest why a great many others have been fascinated by these mammals of the sea. But what the scientists—biologists and psychologists particularly—have tried to find out from the outset is: how "intelligent" are they? Intelligence in any animal is difficult to measure and define, but in cetaceans it is especially so.

In 1948, Arthur F. McBride of Marineland, Florida, and D. O. Hebb of McGill University and Yerkes Laboratory of Primate Biology in Orange Park, Florida, were among the first to try to answer this question. At that time they could come to no final conclusions, but they hoped they could at least clear the way for further systematic studies of porpoise behavior. Let's see what difficulties they encountered in studying what may be called the dolphin's "intelligence," not in comparison with that faculty attributed only to man, but as it is used to describe the "mental capacity" of certain animals we are accustomed to call "intelligent"—for example, dogs or chimpanzees.

First they had to test the ability to learn, but it was not possible to use the same tests that are used on a chimpanzee, for example. These "smart" apes have been taught to roller skate, to use a knife and fork, to ride a bicycle, to climb a ladder, to reach for a banana with a stick, to thread a needle, to light and smoke a cigarette. But porpoises don't have arms, legs, hands, fingers, feet, or toes. Even if tests could be devised suitable to the dolphin's physical equipment, so that its speed of learning could be compared with that of other animals, the rate of learning does not always test intelligence. (Even flatworms can learn to avoid an electric shock by associating it with a light signal.) McBride and Hebb pointed out that certain things may be learned more rapidly by a lower species than by a higher one. Thus a rat can learn to distinguish black from white in from 5 to 10 trials, while it takes a chimpanzee from 200 to 300 trials. (In a test devised by Dr. Lilly and described later on, the dolphin learned one operation in fewer trials than a chimpanzee.)

Then there is the manner or the kind of learning. Lower animals, including insects, learn by trial-and-error, the lowest level of learning. Let's say you were trying to put together a jig-saw puzzle of an animal, a house, or a map of the United States. You could do it in two ways: you could put the pieces together helter-skelter, over and over again, until all fitted into place; or you could examine the shape of the individual pieces and get an idea of which ones should go which way. The second way is called insight, ideational learning, or problem-solving. By this method a chimpanzee, given several sticks of different lengths, will choose the one long enough to enable him to reach a banana on a shelf. Taking this as a standard, would you say that the dolphin who found a way to dislodge the feather sticking to the side of the tank, or the one who used the spine of the scorpion fish to prod the eel out of his corner, was capable of problem-solving?

In the absence of reliable tests, McBride and Hebb decided that the porpoise's "I. Q." might be gauged by observing its behavior under conditions of tank life. They noticed that porpoises characteristically showed fear of strange inanimate objects lowered into the tank: a wooden frame for underwater photography, a raft, a bright-colored plastic ball. They gathered in a tight school as far away from the object as possible. If the object turned out to be the raft with which they were familiar, the school broke up, but if a strange fishing net was lowered, they continued to swim excitedly in a tight group.

Another observation was that porpoises were capable of making strong individual attachments. In one instance, two males that had been captured together stayed close to each other in the tank for about a month. Then one of them was removed to another aquarium for an exhibit. When the porpoise was brought back three weeks later there was a great deal of excitement. "No doubt could exist that the two recognized each other, and for several hours they swam side by side rushing frenziedly through the water, and on several occasions they leaped completely out of the water. For several days, the two males were inseparable and neither paid any attention to the female," McBride reported. The female was a porpoise which, prior to the separation, had been an object of jealousy between the two males, but now they were inseparable, despite the fact that it was the courting season.

Over-all dolphin behavior includes: selective friendship; mutual dependence and schooling during distress and danger; pining for a companion; memory of fearful experiences such as confinement; capacity for sustained interest; inventive, complex, and sustained social play; teasing and minor attacks without injury to shark, pelican, or human; problem-solving; and complex and versatile courtship. By all these characteristics, dolphins were judged to be high among mammals in their development—perhaps placing between the dog and the chimpanzee, and certainly far closer to, if not higher than, the latter.

Observation of their behavior was one means of assessing the dolphin's capabilities. Next came systematic training. In the training of any animal, answering to a stimulus such as the sound of a whistle or a bell, or the turning on of a light, is rewarded with food; failure results in punishment (lack of food or a painful electric shock). It was discovered quite early that dolphins will respond best when rewarded. Let's say that the attendant appeared regularly with a bucket of fish on the feeding platform. To get the dolphin to come to the platform and accept a fish from his hand, the attendant gave a signal—a whistle or handclap—as the "bridging" or "reinforcing" stimulus. Every time the dolphin did what was wanted of him, he got his reward, and soon learned to come when summoned by the "bridging" stimulus.

Trainer in tank with Pigmy Sperm whale as it "walks"

MARINELAND OF FLORIDA

Of course, there are certain "ground rules" for this training "game." The dolphin must be made to feel that the trainer is his friend and will not do him harm, and it helps when the trainer gets into the tank and pets him. And always the dolphin must be rewarded for his correct performance. Also, the dolphin has to have the physical equipment to learn the trick, such as the ability to jump higher and higher for a fish held at an ever-increasing height.

Dr. Lilly tells how one dolphin was trained in the early days in Marineland, Florida. "For Splash to squirt water from his mouth by closing his jaws rapidly near the surface, André's signal was to spit water out of his mouth and tap the side of the tank with his hand. Splash would then squirt the water and André would reward him with a small bit of fish." Apparently the dolphin would cooperate equally well with Dr. Lilly's thirteen-year-old son who, with a whistle and hand signals, trained him to offer a flipper in a handshaking gesture, to jump out of the water, and to catch a football.

Later, when he had transferred his laboratory to St. Thomas in the Virgin Islands, Dr. Lilly used a more sophisticated method of training. It had been known for some time that there were different areas in the brains of rats and monkeys (and by inference in man) concerned with pleasurable and painful feelings. Using a local anesthetic, making the procedure painless, Dr. Lilly inserted fine electrodes into dolphins' brains. The pleasure and pain areas in the brain can be stimulated electrically, bringing about a sense of pleasure or distress, depending upon whether the "positive" or "negative" brain zone is affected. Animals such as rats have been trained to switch on the current by pressing a lever to get a pleasurable sensation, and to turn it off when the pain center is stimulated. Dr. Lilly trained his dolphins to use their snouts to operate such levers and found that they learned the trick quickly. One wild dolphin, newly captured, mastered it after only 20 trials, while it generally takes monkeys at least 100 trials. Here was a test by which the learning ability of the two

Shaking "hands"

species could be compared, and the dolphin outstripped the monkey by far!

A recent dolphin-training experiment was carried out at the Oceanic Institute at Makapuu Point, Waimanalo, Oahu, Hawaii. The dolphin (named Keiki, which is Hawaiian for "child") was a male Pacific bottlenose (*Tursiops gilli*), not fully grown, taken from a school about 30 miles off the coast of Oahu. After a few days of captivity, Keiki learned to respond to a police whistle by being fed fish each time. The reward was always given when he performed correctly—stopping in front of the trainer, for example. And the reward for correct behavior was the only food he was given.

The training was done in a partially enclosed lagoon about 1,000 feet long, where Keiki's "permanent" home was an anchored, floating, chain-link cage. Half the lagoon was blocked off by a net barrier. After two days the cage was opened, and Keiki was let out (after some coaxing) and escorted by swimmers into the full length of the netted lagoon. When he refused to get back into the cage, he was forced back by a "crowder" net, and after three trials he learned to return on command. Keiki was trained to touch an underwater speaker with his snout when the sound was turned on. Gradually, the speaker was moved farther and farther away from him, so that he had to swim toward it and stop directly in front of it. The signal was a train of repeated clicks between 2 and 4 kilocycles a second—a tone high enough to be heard over long distances above the normal background noises of the ocean.

He was then allowed to swim freely in the lagoon; but he returned on command and seldom ventured outside his immediate area. During these excursions his swimming speed was timed. His total food intake measured about 15 pounds of frozen surf smelt a day, varying according to what his training required. He was entirely dependent upon the experimenters for food. On two occasions he was seen to pick up some floating medusas and polyps, but he did not attempt to catch fish, partly because to get his reward he had to keep up his speed and this gave him no time for foraging.

During the first weeks of daily training sessions Keiki was required to leave the cage on cue, swim a 200-foot course at high (16.1 knots) speed and return to his cage upon hearing the recall signal. Then the cage was closed until the next day when the procedure was repeated.

After only a week of training in the cage, the restraining nets were removed so that Keiki was free to go out into the open sea, but he never ventured out alone. On the final day of the experiment, the recall signal speaker was placed on an outboard motored skiff, and Keiki was led by periodic recalls through the lagoon and into the deep channel, but he stayed close to the boat. Once outside the lagoon he "became visibly nervous, exhibiting jaw chattering and tail slapping, and showing the white of the eyes—behavior patterns which have been associated with agitation in cetaceans," Dr. Kenneth Norris reported in an article in *Science,* February 26, 1965. Then after several recalls in the open water he plunged away from the boat and, when he was an estimated 700 feet away, the signal was switched on. He stopped immediately upon picking up the signal and returned directly to the speaker.

Dr. Norris explains that to establish this pattern of learned behavior many factors were involved: controlled feeding, "social ties between the scientist and the porpoise, fear of unknown waters, his isolation in the cage, the systematic training, and becoming accustomed to a single kind of food." (The last has been observed in other captives: you will remember Albert in Dr. Kellogg's experiment.)

To make up for Keiki's isolation, the experimenters often stroked and patted him during and after work sessions, and he responded by allowing himself to be transported when necessary without putting up a struggle. His occasional fright—when he was first taken beyond his accustomed limits, or when he at first refused to go through the gates—is normal for bottlenoses in captivity. They are afraid to go where they cannot see—under unfamiliar objects above water, or over new obstacles placed on the bottom. In these fearful situations the porpoise leaned on his captors for protection.

This experiment in training has certain by-products: other

Above: Pilot whale gets its teeth brushed; Right: North Atlantic Pilot whale jumps completely out of water to beat a punching bag

porpoises have been broken to harness, for example. At the time this is being written there are four more "open sea" porpoises in Hawaii and one in the Point Mugu laboratory. They will not only permit the studying of additional ways to control behavior, but the attaching of instruments for recording heart rate, blood pressure, and respiration as well.

Not only dolphins but also pilot whales have been trained to perform in the Marineland stadia. In Marineland, Florida, two pilot whales, on command, "go to school" (carrying their "books" suspended from a strap), open their monstrous jaws for a throat examination and tooth brushing by "the school doctor," and pull a puppy on a surfboard across the pool. In Marineland of the Pacific, the now famed Bubbles, a 1,500-pound, 14-foot-long female star, leaps a hurdle, beats a punching bag, and waves at the audience with her flippers. In a more lady-like role she dons a flowered bonnet, and "dances" and "sings" a few squeaky tones through her open blowhole.

The hurdle jump started with an observation that Bubbles

Bubbles, Pacific Pilot whale, models her newest bonnet

liked to scratch her belly on a skimmer used to clean the water's surface. And so her trainer, Mr. David H. Brown, decided to gradually raise it until the whale learned to hurdle it.

Pilot whales apparently adapt more easily to captivity, and are more tractable. Although mainly night animals in the wild state, they adjust to daytime activity in the tank, and unlike dolphins, they show little concern over unusual objects in the tank. Mr. Brown writes:

Once I lowered a large dinghy into the tank and, to my surprise, no fear reaction was registered by the whale. She came to the dinghy's side after a few minutes to be fed and even performed several tricks, receiving her cues from the unusual new feeding platform. This comparative lack of fearfulness may be the reason for the pilot whale's rapid response . . . to captivity and human contact.

Their capacity for play is as great as that of the dolphin's, and their tendency to form social groups on which they depend for security is highly developed.

Their lesser physical agility is perhaps due to their less sleek, heavy-set, and relatively inflexible bodies. This body structure is responsible for the pilot whale's preference for squid as food, rather than fish, in contrast to the maneuverable dolphin, better equipped for the pursuit of fast-moving prey. In captivity, pilot whales are less aggressive than dolphins; in mock fights and games of chase with their more active cousins, they are usually on the defensive.

Long before the dolphin was available for intensive study, it was known that all cetaceans had large brains with a highly complex structure. Such facts as the weight of the brain, complexity of the convolutions (folds) in its outer, gray matter, and the degree of development of certain of its sensory centers are clues to the whale's "mental" capacity. From the size and intricacy of the nervous system, the biologist can reasonably judge the development of certain functions, somewhat the way an electronic engineer could judge the complexity of a man-made satellite in space from the complicated ground receiving and guiding center. Even before it was shown that hearing is very well developed in the dolphin, it was known that in toothed whales the auditory nerve is the largest (and in baleens second in size to the optic nerve) of all twelve cranial nerves; the hearing center in the brain is very large, while the part of the brain that deals with the sense of smell is almost entirely lacking. On the other hand, in the dog and fish the olfactory structures in the brain are very well developed. So if we didn't otherwise know that the dog has a good sense of smell, we could surmise it from an examination of its brain.

The brains of many animals, including cetaceans, have been weighed, but brain weight alone would be meaningless in determining mental capacity. If we were to judge merely by weight, the blue whale's 15-pound brain next to man's 3-pound brain would lead to the absurd conclusion that the whale's mental endowment far outreaches that of the human. When, however, we relate brain weight to body weight or body length of animals that are fairly similar in size, we have a more reasonable basis for comparing their mental capacity. In the table below are the figures that have been used for this type of comparison.

	Body Weight in pounds	Brain Weight in pounds and ounces		Percentage of body weight that is brain	Length in feet	Ounces of brain tissue per foot of body length
		Pounds	Ounces	%		
Man	150	3.1	49.6	2.1	5.7	8.5
Dolphin	300	3.5	56	1.17	8	7
Chimpanzee	110	.77	12.5	.7	5	2.5

To understand what these figures mean, you must remember that the weight and the length are averages for different individuals in each species and that they represent only one way of estimating—and a rough estimate it is—the probable mental capacity of the species compared. Keeping these limitations in mind, it would seem that the dolphin's brain (which is actually heavier than man's) is closer to that of man than is the chimpanzee's. Considering body length, man has roughly 8.5 ounces of brain tissue for each foot of his height, the dolphin 7 ounces, and the chimpanzee 2.5 ounces for each foot of body length.

Another method, thought to give a more accurate comparison, is based on the relationship of brain size to the surface area, which is also a rough measure of the metabolism of the animal. And since a large brain requires a high level of metabolism for

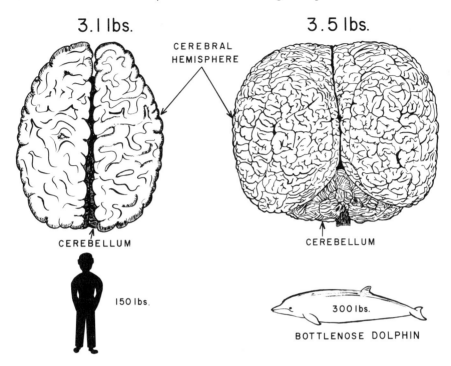

Brain of a man and of a Bottlenose dolphin

proper functioning, Dr. Slijper has put it another way: "We might have guessed that Cetaceans would have a high metabolic rate from the size of their brain alone." But the rorquals are believed to have a low metabolism. At any rate, using this relationship of brain size to surface area, animals have been arranged by one scientist on a scale from 1 to 7. On this scale, modern man is at level 7, earlier races of man are at level 6, toothed whales and chimpanzees at level 5, and baleen whales at level 4.

These figures, suggesting the superior mental capacity of dolphins, bear out the observations on their behavior and on their method and rate of learning. Most animal experimenters, therefore, regard the mental capacity of the dolphin as being close to that of the chimpanzee, and some consider the dolphin ahead of the chimpanzee. Among those who give the dolphin a very high intelligence rating is Dr. John C. Lilly, who believes that it may be possible some day for humans to communicate with the dolphins through "some sort of complex language."

To begin with, Dr. Lilly makes a distinction between "intellectual capacity" and "intelligence." Intelligence, he says, is a word that can be applied to any animal at levels lower than that of humans, but intellectual capacity can be properly applied only to beings that can do more than aping, and are capable of learning to speak and understand a language, however small the vocabulary may be. Thus, a rat can learn the course of a maze (a winding pathway) that leads him toward food or away from a painful shock. Accordingly the rat ranks as "intelligent" in Dr. Lilly's nine levels of "intelligence," but he would place a mentally retarded person who can learn a small vocabulary on the first level of his "intellectual capacity scale."

To attain this level an organism would have to have two physical attributes: a brain of a certain size, which he calls "critical," and the ability to control the necessary muscles for formulating the spoken word. Immediately, we see that dolphins have neither vocal cords to vocalize, nor muscles for speech, using their nasal structures to make the different sounds by which to communicate with each other when in distress or danger, during courtship, and to navigate and seek out food. The brain, however, is phenomenally large, as we know, and on this point Dr. Lilly believes that there may be a "critical absolute brain size below which language, as we know it, is impossible and above which . . . it is possible and even probable." To support his argument he points out that when a human baby says its first word (at the age of about 9 months) its brain has grown from a little over a pound at 2 months to 1.7 pounds. At the age of 23 months, when it begins to use phrases and sentences with pronouns, its brain weight has grown to over 2.1 pounds. At the age of 23 months, the dolphin's brain weighs as much as the human baby's at age 41 months (2.7 pounds).

Dr. Lilly bases his hunch that dolphins may have a language of their own, which he calls "dolphinese," first on the size of their brains, and second on the belief that dolphins can make "humanoid" (human-like) sounds including some that resemble human laughter. In his experiments to test their ability to turn on the switch for the pleasurable sensations they derived, it seemed to him that they made such sounds to express their joy in self-stimulation.

And in 1963 he wrote:

Some of the most interesting information is connected with their ability to make sounds which resemble those emitted by humans during speaking. . . . We have found that if one of these animals is placed in close contact with humans who talk to him every day, eventually he will begin to raise his blowhole up out of the water and make "humanoid" noises in air. (Their normal mode of discourse is underwater.) We find (without the use of electrical stimulation of the brain by means of electrodes) that we can obtain mimicry of several human words ("more," "up," "speak," "squirt," "ok," "yes," etc.).

At the medical meeting previously mentioned, Dr. Lilly reported that in the repetition of nonsense syllables given to them in a row, dolphins did better than humans. While humans can repeat about five or six of the syllables correctly and in proper order, the dolphins could perform this stunt with twelve syllables.

Since Dr. Lilly has literally lived with dolphins for at least eight years and talked to them as to close friends and members of his family, he has learned to recognize their sounds as "primitive copies of our speech." Are they understandable to others, however? Dr. Lilly tells us that since they occur at such high frequency and only for short periods, the untrained listener has difficulty in hearing them. For such persons the recordings on tape must be played back at half or one-fourth the speed, until they learn to detect them. Many cetologists are skeptical about this. And, since further proof is necessary, these sounds have been translated electronically so that they can be "seen" as squiggles photographed from an oscilloscope, just as echo-locating sounds have been recorded. These squiggles can be compared with those made from similarly recorded human sounds.

This work of Dr. Lilly's has not been repeated by other workers, and some scientists are skeptical about "dolphinese." It has been pointed out, for example, that in the various aquaria where, for years, dolphins have repeatedly heard the same sounds —whistle signals and voice commands used in training—they have not generally been known to repeat them. Others have adopted a "wait and see" attitude, maintaining an open mind about the dolphins' ability to communicate with humans. But it would be fair to say that most agree that if such porpoise-human "conversations" should indeed some day be achieved, it will have to be through electronic recording, just as underwater sounds of various kinds have been recorded on magnetic tape. Then, per-haps, a "porpoise language" could be decoded and certain "words" would become intelligible to us.

In the meantime, when we read about dolphins "talking," let's remember that even if it's true they will not be using Eng-lish, French, Japanese, or Russian, but only "dolphinese," transmitted as electronic signals.

12

What's Ahead For Whales?

How marvellously whales are fitted for their way of life! But what does the future hold for them? As huge and powerful as they are, can they survive or, like the giants in the past, will they vanish? The biologist will tell you that no species can grow and multiply unchecked. It is doing well if it can hold its own in the face of catastrophic changes in environment, natural enemies, destruction by man, accidents, and disease.

Whalers will tell you that whales are among the most healthy animals, or so it seems from their inspection of the catch. Still, whales do have diseases, and some of their illnesses are much like those of humans. Whales have been overcome by parasitic roundworms as thin as a cotton thread and less than an inch long. The worms invade the whale through the fish it eats; they get into the whale's air passages, its middle ear, and even into its heart and blood vessels. Sperm whales, particularly, suffer from intestinal parasites such as tapeworms that "sit at its table" and share its food, while others settle in the whale's tissues, infesting large areas of its flesh.

And whales frequently have pneumonia; they suffer from tumors, damaged livers, skin abscesses, infections of the teeth and jaws, and even from a crippling bone disease that deforms their spines. In the Whaling Museum at Mystic, Connecticut, you can see a stone larger than your head, which is said to have been removed from a whale's kidney. If it really was a kidney stone, Dr. John W. Draper, a modern urologist who has examined it, tells us that the whale must have been very sick indeed with a severe kidney infection.

Porpoises can choke on fish. A young Pacific striped porpoise, captured in a small-boat harbor, was treated with antibiotics and vitamins for four days for severe illness—all in vain. Finally it was discovered that a fish was clogging its gullet and forestomach. And it had severe stomach ulcers. Another captive, a Pacific common porpoise stranded on a nearby beach, was found to be infested with cysts of tapeworm larvae, some an inch wide, imbedded in its muscles, abdomen, and brain. The damage to its *cerebellum* caused it to reel crazily and circle until finally it died.

In a recent article in a veterinary journal the following diseases found in dolphins and porpoises were described: soreness of mouth, tongue, and gums; scurvy; loss of appetite; inflammation of the heart sac; skin abscesses; swollen lymph glands; eroded stomach; abrasions of the cornea; pneumonia; and heart disease that caused the death of a beluga whale. The list keeps growing ever longer as more and more cetaceans are taken captive. You remember that Moby Doll, the Vancouver killer whale, had a fungus disease of the skin and, a few years ago, the deadly infection of the skin called erysipelas took the lives of five dolphins in Marineland, Florida.

Only recently a report came from the Sea World Oceanarium, San Diego, California, of the first case of diabetes in a female dolphin. Dr. David W. Kenney, the director of collecting and research there, found that the five-year-old Cyrene became emaciated, lost her appetite, developed a skin irritation and stomach trouble and a cataract in one eye. But the clinching evidence was the laboratory report that she had more than double the normal amount of sugar in the blood. After Dr. Kenney injected Cyrene with a shot of insulin, her blood sugar went down. After two weeks of daily injections, her weight returned to normal and she became her playful self. Then the insulin was replaced by a tablet of a drug that could be fed her inside a mackerel as part of her regular diet. This medicine is keeping her well, and she's back on the "stage show."

Top: Pilot whale being vacci-
nated against erysipelas;
Bottom: Cyrene, the diabetic
dolphin, is given medicine
inside a mackerel

There are, also, all kinds of accidents. Pilot whales die by the score in mass strandings, ironically because they stay in closely knit groups, and follow a leader. If the school is accidentally led close to shore, they are all likely to become beached, because none will leave its companions even though it means death. If they have not migrated south in time, porpoises are sometimes caught in the ice and perish when the Baltic Sea freezes over, and the little piked whale may meet a similar fate if it fails to break a hole through the ice; both perish by being cut off from their air supply.

The strangest of all accidents has been known to happen to sperm whales. Most whales sleep, so to say, "with one eye open," dozing off momentarily, but the sperm whale is reported to be a deep sleeper. Now and then one is "caught napping," a sudden shock is felt aboard ship as if the vessel hit an iceberg head on, but it is only the ship's bow or propeller colliding with a sleeping sperm whale, and sometimes with a California gray whale.

Whales have few natural enemies because their very size and speed of swimming make them superior to all other creatures of the sea. In fights with even the largest sharks they come off the victors with only nicks, scratches, and surface bites as battle scars, although porpoises are sometimes killed. The killer whale preys on some—especially on porpoises and belugas and occasionally on the large baleens whose tongues it seeks as food—but it is no immediate threat to the continued existence of most of the many species.

Schooling habits, mutual help in case of danger, care of their young, and protection of the ailing and injured all favor the preservation of whales. In general, they are thought to live peaceably together, although at times, probably during the mating season, mock or real fighting among some species results in broken bones: that is, naturally mended bones have been found in caught whales. And since some survive several fractures without setting by a surgeon, they must, by and large, be healthy creatures.

Bottlenose dolphin and shark living together in tank

And so it comes down to the fact that their biggest threat and worst enemy is man, the hunter, who braves the gales and icebergs of the Antarctic in pursuit of whales. Man's relentless pursuit of whales for food and profit may well mean their extinction. This almost happened to the Biscayan and Greenland right whales, the California grays, and the humpbacks. More than a century ago, Melville wondered "whether Leviathan can long endure so wide a chase, and so remorseless a havoc; whether he must not at last be exterminated from the waters." Yet with all the covetous eyes on the riches to be derived from the whale, man has been forced to call a halt to its destruction.

Alarmed over the virtual disappearance of some species of

Greenland and North Atlantic whales, the whaling magnates have instituted steps to save the disappearing herds. By international agreement they have set rules concerning the number of whale units that may be taken, and the time of year during which whales may be hunted. To check their own greed they have arranged for inspection of whaling ships, and they have ordered punitive measures against wanton killing of "the goose that lays the golden egg." The International Whaling Commission is the modern game warden overseeing the preservation of the oceans' giants.

We have seen that the California gray whale made a comeback with protection by whaling agreements since 1937. Prior to that time, the Norwegians hunted them in 1920, the Russians between 1930 and 1934; and of course, in the previous century they had been hunted almost to extinction.

In 1963, two Biscayan right whales were sighted in the Gulf of Mexico. This species, *Eubalaena glacialis,* a temperate—and subpolar—zone whale, was never before known to enter the Gulf of Mexico. The authors of the article in *Science* thought that this indicated a comeback from 1929, when by international agreement they were to be protected from commercial whaling.

It would seem, then, that except for man's intervention, whales have just about everything in favor of their survival. The oceans are vast, the food is abundant, and the competition from other animals is almost non-existent. And while they produce only one calf about every other year, the year-long nursing and training by the mother helps to preserve the species, and has so far made up for the ravages of disease and accident.

But we can see from the geologic calendar, on which time is measured in millions of years, that many other living things have appeared and disappeared. It is possible that whales will reach a peak of changes and growth and then become extinct.

Many scientists believe that the great whales, at least, are close to their peak now. Their very size limits their further growth. If the blue whale should grow any larger, its circulation might not be adequate to supply its tissues with oxygen and food. And its very specialization, which makes its feeding so effortless, may some day spell its doom. The toothed whales have some advantage over the plankton eaters in that their appetites are more varied.

To be sure, it isn't likely that the seas will dry up, or the ocean's food disappear. But suppose a change of climate such as a geologic heat wave did warm up the polar caps, or that a change in the ocean's current drove away the krill, or even caused it to disappear from the Antarctic. What would happen to the blue whale?

Will the whale of today follow the dinosaur of yesterday?

Which Whale Is Which?

THE TABLE THAT FOLLOWS (beginning on page 242) gives the common and scientific names of the whales, dolphins, and porpoises you have read about in this book.

The long, scientific Latin names, that are often confusing, are full of meaning for the scientist because they not only identify the animal, but place it in a group that shows its relationship to others in a larger group.

The names are in Latin because at one time this was the language of all learned men. To avoid writing impossibly long descriptions of every living thing, naturalists gave each plant and animal an appropriate name and tried to classify them. Beginning with Aristotle, they have tried to bring order out of chaos by grouping the millions of different kinds according to certain characteristics.

The most important classifier was the Swede, Carl von Linne, better known as Linnaeus. In the eighteenth century he established what is known as the binomial, or two-name, system. Just as people have at least two names—James Jones—all living things were named by genus and species: *Tursiops truncatus* (always in italics) for the Atlantic bottlenose dolphin. *Tursiops gilli*, a different bottlenose species found in the Pacific, is a close relative and therefore has the same genus name.

Related genera, in turn, are grouped into families. Thus, *Balaenoptera acutorostrata*, the little piked whale, belongs to the family of *Balaenopteridae*, the scientific name for rorquals. (The *ae* ending stands for the family name.) You can see from the table that these whales belong to the suborder of *Mysticetes*, or

240

baleen whales. And then from the "distinctive feature" column you can tell what a *Balaenoptera acutorostrata* looks like.

An "L" after a scientific name stands for Linnaeus; otherwise, as shown, either Cope, Gray, or Cuvier named the particular species.

Where there are two names, one is given in parentheses: the killer whale is *Orcinus orca* and also *Orcinus rectipinna,* because it was named by two different scientists. Also, some whales have more than one common name: the blue whale is also "sulphurbottom"; the Greenland right whale is also "bowhead" and "great polar whale." Where "a," "b," or "c" is given, it means that these are different species.

In the table we have followed the names as listed by Dr. Slijper in his book *Whales,* and by Victor B. Scheffer and Dale W. Rice of the Bureau of Commercial Fisheries, U.S. Fish and Wildlife Service, Seattle, Washington. As the latter authors say, ". . . any list of marine mammals, especially of smaller cetaceans, can only be regarded as extremely provisional." So, if you see new or additional names elsewhere, do not be surprised.

MYSTACOCETI—MYSTICETES—WHALEBONE WHALES
BALEEN WHALES

Whalebone in mouth. No teeth in adult. Lower jaw wide, jawbones arch outwards. Skull symmetrical. Double blowholes.

A. Right Whales   Balaenidae
No dorsal fin   No throat grooves   Long whalebone

COMMON NAME	SCIENTIFIC NAME	LENGTH FEET AVER-AGE	LENGTH FEET MAXI-MUM	WHERE FOUND	PREVALENCE AND DISTINCTIVE FEATURES
1. Greenland right (bowhead)	Balaena mysticetus	50	51	Arctic Ocean, Bering and Okhotsk Seas	Rare and protected by international law
2. Biscayan right	Eubalaena glacialis	48		All oceans except tropical	Fairly rare and protected by international law
3. Pigmy right	Caperea marginata	19		Antarctic Ocean off New Zealand, Australia, S. Amer.	Fairly rare and protected by international law

B. Gray Whale   Eschrichtiidae (Rhachianectidae)
No dorsal fin   2-4 grooves   Short baleen

COMMON NAME	SCIENTIFIC NAME	LENGTH FEET AVER-AGE	LENGTH FEET MAXI-MUM	WHERE FOUND	PREVALENCE AND DISTINCTIVE FEATURES
1. California gray (devil fish) (mussel-digger)	Eschrichtius gibbosus (Erxleben) Eschrichtius glaucus (Cope) Rhachianectes glaucus (old name)	41	45	N. Pacific	Gray patches due to concentration of barnacles Scarce and protected Dorsal fin absent

C. Rorquals Balaenopteridae
Short baleen Dorsal fin 40-100 grooves

COMMON NAME	SCIENTIFIC NAME	LENGTH FEET AVERAGE	MAXIMUM	WHERE FOUND	PREVALENCE AND DISTINCTIVE FEATURES
1. Blue (sulphur-bottom)	Balaenoptera musculus	80	100	All oceans Largely in cold waters	Dorsal fin very small and far back. Bluish-gray; mottled; underside of flipper is white
2. Fin (finner) (finback) (common rorqual)	Balaenoptera physalus	68	70	All oceans	Black above and white below. Grooves extend about half the length of body
3. Sei (coal fish) (pollack)	Balaenoptera borealis	46	55	All oceans	Black above, shading to bluish gray. Flippers and flukes never white on underside. Blow is small
4. Bryde's	Balaenoptera brydei (Olsen) Balaenoptera edeni (Anderson)	42		Tropics and sub-tropics	Very much like sei whale
5. Little piked (lesser rorqual) (Minke) (sharp-headed finner)	Balaenoptera acutorostrata	30	30	All oceans; less frequent in tropics	Black on back; white on underside
6. Humpback (bunch) (hump)	Megaptera novaengliae	45	50	All oceans	Thick and bulky body; long and narrow flippers with knobs along edges. Fewer throat grooves than in other rorquals and widely spaced

ODONTOCETI (Toothed Whales)

Teeth of uniform type present in adults; sometimes buried in gums. Whalebone absent. Single blowhole. The skull is asymmetrical.

COMMON NAME	SCIENTIFIC NAME	LENGTH FEET AVER-AGE	MAXI-MUM	WHERE FOUND	PREVALENCE AND DISTINCTIVE FEATURES
A. Sperm Whales Physeteriidae	Cuttlefish eaters. Usually teeth in upper jaws are hidden in gums.				
1. Sperm (cachelot) (pot-head) (spermaceti whale)	Physeter catodon (L.) Physeter macrocephalus (L.)	Male 51-60 Female 38		All oceans	Large square head. Blowhole on left side in front of head. Bushy blow directed obliquely forward. Fluke raised during dive
2. Pigmy sperm	a. Kogia breviceps b. Kogia simus	9	13	All oceans	Bluntly conical snout. Black above, grayish white below, Blowhole left of midline
B. Beaked Whales Ziphiidae	Pointed beak. Two longitudinal grooves on throat. Rudimentary teeth, except in Tasmacetus. Cuttlefish eaters.				
1. Bottlenose whale	a. Hyperoodon ampullatus Hyperoodon rostratus b. Hyperoodon planifrons	30		North Atlantic Antarctic; South Pacific	Prominent forehead. 6-7 inch beak in males. Front end of lower jaw fused Close relative of Atlantic bottlenose whale.
2. Sowerby a. beaked whale b. Gulf Stream beaked whale	a. Mesoplodon bidens b. Mesoplodon europaeus M. gervaisi	13	22	North Atlantic Tropical and near tropical North Atlantic	

COMMON NAME	SCIENTIFIC NAME	LENGTH FEET AVERAGE	MAXIMUM	WHERE FOUND	PREVALENCE AND DISTINCTIVE FEATURES
3. Baird's beaked whale	a. Berardius bairdi	Males 30 Females 42	39	North Pacific	Largest of beaked whales. Gray to black with some white markings on underside
	b. Berardius arnouxi			In southern hemisphere	Close relative to Berardius bairdi
4. Cuvier's Beaked whale (goose-beaked whale)	Ziphius carvirostris	26 Females slightly larger	27	All oceans	Head slopes gently backwards. Beak short. Single pair of teeth visible at tip of lower jaw in males, but buried in gums of females
5. Tasmacetus	Tasmacetus shepherdi			New Zealand waters	Functioning teeth in both jaws

C. Ocean Dolphins   Delphinidae (In the wider sense)

Mainly fish eaters. Lower jaws fused only at tip.

COMMON NAME	SCIENTIFIC NAME	LENGTH FEET AVERAGE	MAXIMUM	WHERE FOUND	PREVALENCE AND DISTINCTIVE FEATURES
1. Beluga whale (white whale)	Delphinapterus leucas	14	15	Arctic Ocean and adjacent seas	Adults pure white. Slate-blue during 1st year, then changes to gray, light blue, and finally white at 4-5 years. No dorsal fin
2. Narwhal	Monodon monoceros	13	16	Atlantic sector Arctic Ocean	Spirally twisted tooth in male; extends 8-9 feet from head. Formerly hunted for ivory of tusk, oil

D. Porpoises (Phocaenidae)
Usually clear dorsal fin. No back. Teeth spade-shaped.

COMMON NAME	SCIENTIFIC NAME	LENGTH FEET AVERAGE	MAXIMUM	WHERE FOUND	PREVALENCE AND DISTINCTIVE FEATURES
1. Common porpoise (harbor porpoise)	Phocoena phocoena / Phocoena vomerina	4½	6	North Atlantic North Pacific	Blunt snout / No beak
2. Dall's porpoise	a. Phocoenoides dalli	to 6		North Pacific	Sharp contrast of white side patches against slate gray to black. Hump above the tail. Seen in bow wave of ships
	b. Phocoenoides truei			Japanese waters	Relative of Phocoenoides dalli
3. Finless Black porpoise	Neophocaena phocaenoides	4		South East Asia	Almost entirely black. Lacks a dorsal fin

E. Dolphins in the Stricter Sense (Delphinidae Sensu Stricto)
Usually clear dorsal fin; some cervical vertebrae generally fused. Conical teeth; usually beaked.

COMMON NAME	SCIENTIFIC NAME	LENGTH FEET AVERAGE	MAXIMUM	WHERE FOUND	PREVALENCE AND DISTINCTIVE FEATURES
1. Killer (Pacific killer)	Orcinus orca (L.) / Orcinus rectipinna (Cope)	Male 22 / Female 19	30	All oceans Chiefly focal	Conspicuous white markings. High triangular dorsal fin. Only one that preys on warm-blooded animals
2. False Killer whale	Pseudorca crassidens	16	18	All oceans except polar	Body more slender, flippers narrower, fin smaller than in true killer. All black

COMMON NAME	SCIENTIFIC NAME	LENGTH FEET AVERAGE	MAXIMUM	WHERE FOUND	PREVALENCE AND DISTINCTIVE FEATURES
3. Pilot whale (blackfish)	Globicephala scammoni (Cope) Globicephala sieboldi (Gray)		Males 20 Fe-males 16	North Pacific	Bulbous forehead. Short beak. Usually entirely black. Short fin. Flippers long and narrow. Travels in large schools. Often stranded in large numbers
	Globicephala (Traill) melaena			North Atlantic	
	Globicephala macrorhyncha (Gray)			Tropical Atlantic Indian Oceans	
Pacific pilot whale	Globicephala scammoni (Cope)	26		North Pacific	
4. Risso's	Grampus griseus (no relationship to killer)	10	13	Northern & Southern hemispheres	Lacks well-defined beak. Gray and white on back; almost white underside; conspicuous white streaks on back
5. Common dolphin ("saddle-back")	a. Delphinus delphis (L.) b. Delphinus delphis bairdi (Dall) c. Delphinus delphis ponticus (Barabash)	7		Everywhere except very cold waters	Black on the back, white underside, gray last third of back to fluke
6. White-sided dolphin (Pacific striped dolphin) Several species in North Atlantic; tropics; southern waters	Langenorhynchus obliquidens (Gill) Langenorhynchus thicolea (Gray)	5	10	North Pacific	Beak short and poorly defined. Black back with white stripes, and white on sides. Schools of 30 and 40 play at bow of a ship

COMMON NAME	SCIENTIFIC NAME	LENGTH FEET AVER-AGE	MAXI-MUM	WHERE FOUND	PREVALENCE AND DISTINCTIVE FEATURES
7. a. Long-snouted	Stenella styx	10		North Atlantic	Both long-snouted (beak long and narrow). Some are spotted—light gray on black
b. Spotted dolphin	Stenella graffmani (Lönnberg) Stenella plagiodon (Cope)			West Coast of North America	
8. a. Northern right whale dolphin	Lissodelphis borealis	5½	8	North Pacific	Complete absence of dorsal fin. Short beak. Black nearly all over; white between flippers and underside of fluke
b. Southern right whale dolphin	Lissodelphis peroni			Related species in southern seas	
9. Bottlenose dolphin (Atlantic bottlenose dolphin) (porpoise in U.S.)	a. Tursiops truncatus	5	8	North Atlantic	Well-defined snout. Moderately high dorsal fin. Gray; white on throat and belly
Pacific bottlenose dolphin	b. Tursiops gilli	8	10	Central Pacific to equator	Uniform brownish gray
10. Irrawaddy dolphin	Orcaella brevirostris	7		South East Asia Coast	

F. River Dolphins (Platanistidae)

River inhabitants.   Very long slender beaks.   Lower jaws fused over larger area.

COMMON NAME	SCIENTIFIC NAME	LENGTH FEET AVER-AGE	MAXI-MUM	WHERE FOUND	PREVALENCE AND DISTINCTIVE FEATURES
1. Susu or Gangetic dolphin	Platanista gangetica	8		Ganges and Indus Rivers	
2. Boutu or Amazonian dolphin	Inia geoffrensis	6½		Amazon	

BOOKS AND ARTICLES ABOUT WHALES AND
WHALING; DOLPHINS AND PORPOISES

A Captive Whale of Ill Repute. Lovable Killer, *Life,* Nov. 6, 1964.

Alpers, Antony: Dolphins. *The Myth and The Mammal,* Houghton Mifflin, Boston, Mass., 1961.

Andrews, Roy Chapman: *All About Whales,* Random House, New York, 1954.

Anonymous: Saved by a Porpoise, *Natural History,* Nov., 1949.

Appel, Frederic C.: The Intellectual Mammal The Status Pet, *Saturday Evening Post,* Jan. 4–11, 1964.

Ash, Christopher: *Whaler's Eye,* Macmillan, New York, 1962.

Ballantine, Bill: Bubbles: The Educated Whale, *Holiday,* May, 1962.

Blond, George: *The Great Story of Whales,* Hanover House, Garden City, New York, 1955.

Burton, Maurice: *In Their Element. The Story of Water Mammals,* Abelard-Schuman, New York, 1960.

Chapin, Henry: *The Remarkable Dolphin,* William R. Scott, New York, 1962.

Clarke, Arthur A.: Did the Whale Really Swallow Jonah? *Holiday,* March, 1962.

Clever Comics of the Sea, *Life,* Feb. 16, 1959.

Cromie, William J.: The Killer Whale—Wolf of the Seas, *Rod & Gun,* Sept., 1962.

Davis, Egerton Y., Jr.: Man in Whale, *Natural History,* June, 1947.

Essapian, Frank S.: The Birth and Growth of a Porpoise, *Natural History,* Nov., 1953.

Gilmore, Raymond M.: The Return of the Gray Whale, *Scientific American,* Jan., 1955.

Gray, William B., Capt.: *Porpoise Tales,* A. S. Barnes, New York, 1964.

Kay, Helen: *The Secrets of the Dolphin,* Macmillan, New York, 1964.

Lilly, John C.: *Man and Dolphin,* Doubleday, Garden City, New York, 1961.

MacDonald, David: The Saga of Moby Doll, *Rod & Gun,* March, 1965.

McBride, Arthur F.: Meet Mr. Porpoise, *Natural History,* Jan., 1940.

Pequegnat, Willis E.: Whales, Plankton and Man, *Scientific American,* Jan., 1958.

Robertson, R. B.: *Of Whales and Men,* Alfred A. Knopf, New York, 1954.

Ruud, Johan T.: The Blue Whale, *Scientific American,* June, 1956.
            The Giant Whale, *Life,* Aug. 2, 1963.

Walker, Theodore J.: *Whale Primer,* Cabrillo Historical Association, 1962.

Whale Cardiogram, *Scientific American,* Oct., 1952.

White, P. D. and Matthews, S. W.: Hunting the Heartbeat of a Whale, *National Geographic,* July, 1956.

Yoo-Hoo to Namu the Whale, *Sports Illustrated,* July 12, 26, 1965.

ACKNOWLEDGMENTS

THE AUTHORS are deeply indebted, first of all, to the three experts who, by their critical reading of the manuscript, helped to straighten out some of the discrepancies in the literature, and to point up inevitable and friendly disagreements among researchers in the fast-moving, rapidly changing biological story of whales. The three are: Professor Dr. E. J. Slijper, Director, Zoological Laboratorium, University of Amsterdam, President of the Netherlands Whale Research Group, a world authority, whose book *Whales: The Biology of Cetaceans,* is an indispensable item on the bookshelf of all who deal with whales, large and small; Dr. Kenneth S. Norris, Associate Professor of Zoology, University of California, Los Angeles, also of world eminence in dolphin research, which he is conducting at the Oceanic Institute, Oahu, Hawaii; and Dr. Theodore J. Walker, Scripps Institution of Oceanography, University of California, San Diego. With painstaking care, all contributed toward making this a more accurate story; for possible errors and as yet irreconcilable disagreements, the authors take full responsibility.

Invaluable help came from the leaders of the oceanaria visited by the authors: Captain William B. Gray, Director of Collections and Exhibits at the Miami Seaquarium, Florida; Mr. Bruce Bell of Aquarama, Philadelphia, Pennsylvania; and Mr. Clifford Townsend of Marineland, St. Augustine, Florida. Mr. Townsend and Mr. Richard W. Edgerton of Marineland were especially generous in preparing the beautiful photographs of their lovable charges in that aquarium.

Among the many who sent reprints, suggested the initial bibliographic sources, and started the chain of correspondence with experts, the following merit special mention: Dr. F. C. Fraser, Keeper of Zoology, British Museum (Natural History), London; Dr. Demorest Davenport, Chairman of Department of Biological Sciences, University of California, Santa Barbara; Dr. Henry Kritzler, Associate Professor of Biology, Bard College, Annandale-on-Hudson, New York; Frank S. Essapian, Communications Research Institute of St. Thomas, Miami; Dr. Robert C. Boice, Cetacean Research Laboratory, Torrance, California; Dr. C. E. Rice, Stanford Research Institute, Menlo Park, California; Donald W. Wilkie, Director, Aquarium-Museum, University of California, San Diego; C. Clifford Carl, Provincial Museum, Department of Recreation and Conservation, Victoria, B.C.; and F. G. Wood, Jr., Head Marine Sciences Division, U.S. Naval Missile Center, Point Mugu, California.

We are grateful to Dr. William Medway, of the School of Veterinary Medicine, University of Pennsylvania, for both materials and illuminating conversations and correspondence, to Mr. Gary P. Boyker of the Seattle Public Aquarium, Seattle, Washington, for materials, and to whale enthusiast Mr. Christopher Ash for his priceless pictures.

One who helped as much as any to make the book clearer for the reader is Mr. Thomas Danielian, who provided the illuminating original drawings. The authors are also happy to give thanks to Mrs. Reina Hamilton and Mr. Irving Detzger, who for months were doggedly on the trail of library materials; to the librarians of the American Museum of Natural History and Harvard's Museum of Comparative Zoology, Cambridge, Mass., for photostats; and to Mrs. June Jackson for her patience and care in the innumerable retypings of the manuscript.

To all others who tirelessly clipped newspaper items of current interest, and helped in innumerable ways, but who for reasons of space must remain unnamed, our sincere appreciation.

We are also grateful to the following for permission to use photographs: Edward I. Griffin, director, Seattle Public Aquarium, for the pictures on pages 15 and 16; Captain William Gray, Miami Seaquarium, for the pictures on pages 19 (not otherwise credited), 21, 47, 113, 211, and 222, and for those on pages 41 and 114 (photos by Anita Conklin), and for the picture on page 66 (top) (photo by Mike Davis); Dr. William Medway, School of Veterinary Medicine, University of Pennsylvania, and the *American Journal of Physiology,* for the picture on page 32, from W. Medway & J. R. Garaci: Hematology of the Bottlenose Dolphin (*Tursiops truncatus*), *Amer. J. Physiology,* 207:1367, 1964, fig. 1; Mr. Christopher E. Ash, Edinburgh, Scotland, for the pictures on pages

39, 50, 58 (bottom), 107, 108, 109, 111, and 154; New York Zoological Society for the picture on page 42; Aquarama, Theater of the Sea, Philadelphia, for the pictures on pages 47, 99, 144, 185, and on page 225 (right) (Photo by Edwards Vilnis); Chicago Natural History Museum for the pictures on pages 53 and 133; The Marine Historical Association, Inc., Mystic, Conn. (courtesy of Dr. John W. Draper) for the picture on page 61; U. S. Dep't of the Interior, Nat'l Park Service, Cabrillo and Channel Islands National Monuments, San Diego, Calif., for the picture on page 65; U.S. Dep't of the Interior, Fish and Wildlife Service, for the picture on page 81 (photo by Dr. Raymond M. Gilmore); L. Irving, P. F. Scholander, and S. W. Grinnell, *J. Cell. Comp. Physiol.*, 17: 145, from figures 10 and 11, for the picture on page 77; R. L. King, J. L. Jenks, Jr., and P. D. White, Figures 1 & 3 in "The Electrocardiogram of a Beluga Whale" in *Circulation,* 8: 387, September 1953, by permission of Dr. R. L. King and the American Heart Association, Inc. for the picture on page 89; Dr. Alfred W. Senft and Dr. J. Kanwisher, Woods Hole, Mass., for the picture on page 92; The American Heart Association, Inc. for figure 1 from "Cardiographic Observations on a Fin-Back Whale" by Senft and Kanwisher, *Circulation Research* 8: 961, September 1960, for the picture on page 93; Marineland of the Pacific, Palos Verdes, Calif. for the pictures on pages 94 and 138, and on pages 226 and 235 (top) (Photos by Cliff Brown); Fisheries Research Board of Canada, Ottawa, Photos from Bulletin 132 by D. E. Sergeant, on pages 148 and 149; Wm. E. Schevill and B. Lawrence, *J. Exp. Zool.*, 124: 150 & 157, from Figure 1 and Figure 2, for the pictures on page 181; David W. Kenney, D. V. M., "Theatre of the Sea," Sea World, an Oceanarium in San Diego, Calif., for the picture on page 235 (bottom).

Jerome F. Connolly drew the whale pictures on pages 12, 18, 37, 42, 58 (top), 117, 119, 120, and 155.

All pictures not acknowledged above were either drawn by Thomas Danielian, or are acknowledged below the picture itself.

Jacket illustrations are from Marineland of Florida, and jacket design is by Peter Oldenburg.

S.R.R.
E.T.G.

INDEX

Abdomen, 142, 147

Adaptation, of cetaceans:
  to aquatic life, 23, 30, 49, 74, 96;
  in captivity, 48;
  compared with land animals, 27;
  compared with other water mammals, 29, 30;
  see also Evolution

Adrenal glands, 139–140

After-birth (*see* Placenta)

Age estimation, 110, 148, 157

Air sacs, 82, *see also* Lungs

Albinos, 42
  dolphin, *see* Snowball
  whale, *see* Moby Dick

Algae, 104

Alpers, Antony, 44–45, 78, 209

Amazonian dolphin, *see* Boutu

Ambergris, 125

American Museum of Natural History, 37, 125

Amniotic fluid, 164

Amphibians, 26, 27, 28

Ancestors, of whales, 23, 25–49, 111

Andrews, Roy Chapman, 35, 37, 118, 150

Archaeocetes, 34, 171, *see also* Ancestors

Aristotle, on:
  blowhole, 25

Aristotle, on: (Cont.)
  cetaceans, classification of, 25, 240
  dolphins: hearing, 176; sleeping, 34; sounds emitted, 187; suckling, 25; swimming speed, 68

Arteries, *see* Blood vessels

Atlantic bottlenose dolphin, *see* Bottlenose dolphins

Auditory brain centers, *see* Brain

Auditory nerves, 80

Auditory ossicles, *see* Ear, structure of

Backbone, 32, 56, 66, 67

Balaena mysticetus, 242, *see also* Greenland right whale

Balaenidae, 242, *see also* Right whales

Balaenoptera acutorostrata, 243, *see also* Little Piked whale

Balaenoptera borealis, 243, *see also* Sei whale

Balaenoptera brydei, 243, *see also* Bryde's whale

Balaenoptera musculus, 243, *see also* Blue whale

Balaenoptera ocutorostrata, 240, 241, 243, *see also* Little Piked whale

Balaenoptera physalus, 243, *see also* Fin whale

255